THE FALL OF CRETE 1941: WAS FREYBERG CULPABLE?

A thesis presented to the Faculty of the U.S. Army
Command and General Staff College in partial
fulfillment of the requirements for the
degree

MASTER OF MILITARY ART AND SCIENCE
Military History

by

JAMES C. BLISS, MAJ, NEW ZEALAND ARMY
BAL, University of New England, Armidale, NSW, Australia, 2002

Fort Leavenworth, Kansas
2006

Approved for public release; distribution is unlimited.

Report Documentation Page		Form Approved OMB No. 0704-0188

Public reporting burden for the collection of information is estimated to average 1 hour per response, including the time for reviewing instructions, searching existing data sources, gathering and maintaining the data needed, and completing and reviewing the collection of information. Send comments regarding this burden estimate or any other aspect of this collection of information, including suggestions for reducing this burden, to Washington Headquarters Services, Directorate for Information Operations and Reports, 1215 Jefferson Davis Highway, Suite 1204, Arlington VA 22202-4302. Respondents should be aware that notwithstanding any other provision of law, no person shall be subject to a penalty for failing to comply with a collection of information if it does not display a currently valid OMB control number.

1. REPORT DATE **16 JUN 2006**	2. REPORT TYPE	3. DATES COVERED
4. TITLE AND SUBTITLE **Fall of Crete 1941: was Freyberg culpable?**		5a. CONTRACT NUMBER
		5b. GRANT NUMBER
		5c. PROGRAM ELEMENT NUMBER
6. AUTHOR(S) **James Bliss**		5d. PROJECT NUMBER
		5e. TASK NUMBER
		5f. WORK UNIT NUMBER
7. PERFORMING ORGANIZATION NAME(S) AND ADDRESS(ES) **US Army Command and General Staff College,1 Reynolds Ave.,Fort Leavenworth,KS,66027-1352**		8. PERFORMING ORGANIZATION REPORT NUMBER **ATZL-SWD-GD**
9. SPONSORING/MONITORING AGENCY NAME(S) AND ADDRESS(ES)		10. SPONSOR/MONITOR'S ACRONYM(S)
		11. SPONSOR/MONITOR'S REPORT NUMBER(S)

12. DISTRIBUTION/AVAILABILITY STATEMENT
Approved for public release; distribution unlimited.

13. SUPPLEMENTARY NOTES
The original document contains color images.

14. ABSTRACT
On 20 May 1941, Generaloberst Kurt Student?s Luftwaffe XI Fliegerkorps conducted the first operational airborne invasion in history to seize Crete. Major-General Bernard Cyril Freyberg VC, 2nd New Zealand Expeditionary Force, commanded the British forces defending the island. Freyberg, forewarned of the details of the invasion, possessed numerical superiority over the enemy, but was defeated within twelve days. Freyberg, later blamed for the defeat due to his perceived faulty defensive dispositions, was dealt a losing hand from the start. His troops consisted of those that could be rescued from the failed Greek Campaign and lacked sufficient weapons, communications, and transport to conduct the defense. Despite the best efforts of the Royal Navy, overwhelming Luftwaffe air superiority in the absence of the Royal Air Force isolated Crete and the relentless drive of the attacking German forces captured it. Poor tactical leadership by Freyberg?s subordinate commanders and their failure to prosecute his operational plan led to defeat by the barest margin. While a tactical loss, Freyberg?s destruction of the 7th Flieger Division resulted in Hitler never considering an operational airborne assault again. Freyberg, although accepting responsibility for the defeat, should not be held entirely culpable for the loss of Crete.

15. SUBJECT TERMS

16. SECURITY CLASSIFICATION OF:			17. LIMITATION OF ABSTRACT	18. NUMBER OF PAGES	19a. NAME OF RESPONSIBLE PERSON
a. REPORT **unclassified**	b. ABSTRACT **unclassified**	c. THIS PAGE **unclassified**	**1**	**164**	

Standard Form 298 (Rev. 8-98)
Prescribed by ANSI Std Z39-18

MASTER OF MILITARY ART AND SCIENCE

THESIS APPROVAL PAGE

Name of Candidate: MAJ James C. Bliss

Thesis Title: The Fall of Crete 1941: Was Freyberg Culpable?

Approved by:

_____, Thesis Committee Chair
Mr. Wilburn E. Meador, M.A.

_____, Member
Christopher R. Gabel, Ph.D.

_____, Member
Lieutenant Colonel Andrew F. Mahoney, M.S.

Accepted this 16th day of June 2006 by:

_____, Director, Graduate Degree Programs
Robert F. Baumann, Ph.D.

The opinions and conclusions expressed herein are those of the student author and do not necessarily represent the views of the U.S. Army Command and General Staff College or any other governmental agency. (References to this study should include the foregoing statement.)

ABSTRACT

THE FALL OF CRETE 1941: WAS FREYBERG CULPABLE? by MAJ James Bliss, 159 pages.

On 20 May 1941, Generaloberst Kurt Student's Luftwaffe XI Fliegerkorps conducted the first operational airborne invasion in history to seize Crete. Major-General Bernard Cyril Freyberg VC, 2nd New Zealand Expeditionary Force, commanded the British forces defending the island. Freyberg, forewarned of the details of the invasion, possessed numerical superiority over the enemy, but was defeated within twelve days. Freyberg, later blamed for the defeat due to his perceived faulty defensive dispositions, was dealt a losing hand from the start. His troops consisted of those that could be rescued from the failed Greek Campaign and lacked sufficient weapons, communications, and transport to conduct the defense. Despite the best efforts of the Royal Navy, overwhelming Luftwaffe air superiority in the absence of the Royal Air Force isolated Crete and the relentless drive of the attacking German forces captured it. Poor tactical leadership by Freyberg's subordinate commanders and their failure to prosecute his operational plan led to defeat by the barest margin. While a tactical loss, Freyberg's destruction of the 7th Flieger Division resulted in Hitler never considering an operational airborne assault again. Freyberg, although accepting responsibility for the defeat, should not be held entirely culpable for the loss of Crete.

TABLE OF CONTENTS

Page

MASTER OF MILITARY ART AND SCIENCE THESIS APPROVAL PAGE ii

ABSTRACT iii

ACRONYMS v

CHAPTER 1. INTRODUCTION 1

CHAPTER 2. OPERATIONAL ENVIRONMENT 9

CHAPTER 3. OPERATION MERKUR 34

CHAPTER 4. FREYBERG'S OPERATIONAL PLAN 59

CHAPTER 5. THE BATTLE 89

CHAPTER 6. AFTERMATH AND CONCLUSION 127

APPENDIX A. MAP OF THE EASTERN MEDITERRANEAN 139

APPENDIX B. MAP OF CRETE 140

APPENDIX C. GERMAN ORDER OF BATTLE (OPERATION MERKUR) 141

APPENDIX D. OPERATION MERKUR PLAN 143

APPENDIX E. ULTRA SIGNALS 144

APPENDIX F. CREFORCE OPERATION ORDER 148

APPENDIX G. CREFORCE ORDER OF BATTLE 151

APPENDIX H. CREFORCE OPERATIONAL PLAN 153

BIBLIOGRAPHY 154

INITIAL DISTRIBUTION LIST 157

CERTIFICATION FOR MMAS DISTRIBUTION STATEMENT 158

ACRONYMS

AA	Anti Aircraft
ANZAC	Australia New Zealand Army Corps
Aust	Australia/Australian
CinC	Commander in Chief
CREFORCE	Crete Forces
BEF	British Expeditionary Force
DSO	Distinguished Service Order
GOC	General Officer in Charge
HQ	Headquarters
LAYFORCE	Laycock Force
MC	Military Cross
MG	Machine Gun
MNBDO	Mobile Naval Base Defense Organisation
NZ	New Zealand
NZEF	New Zealand Expeditionary Force
OKW	Oberkommando der Wehrmacht (German High Command of the Armed Forces)
RAF	Royal Air Force
RE	Royal Engineers
RN	Royal Navy
UK	United Kingdom
VC	Victoria Cross
W FORCE	Wilson Force

CHAPTER 1

INTRODUCTION

In May 1941, British Middle East Command faced considerable threats to the Mediterranean and North Africa regions. British Forces had achieved decisive victories against the numerically superior Italian Army in Ethiopia and Somaliland in late 1940 and early 1941, and were poised to take Libya. However, in January 1941 *Generalleutnant* Erwin Rommel and his *Deutsches Afrika Korps* intervened to support the Italian forces in North Africa. By the end of March 1941, Rommel had forced the withdrawal of British forces from most of Libya. When Adolph Hitler attacked into Greece and Yugoslavia in April 1941 to secure his southeastern flank for his upcoming operations against the Soviet Union, the British government directed Commander-in-Chief (CinC), Middle East Command General Sir Archibald Percival Wavell[1] to commit troops in support of the Greek mainland.

The Battle of Greece was a decisive defeat for the British and Greek forces. In little over three weeks, the Germans attacked through Bulgaria into Yugoslavia and Greece, and forced the withdrawal of approximately 57,000 Allied troops. Of these, some redeployed to North Africa with the remainder to the garrison on the Greek island of Crete. Crete occupied a strategic position within the Mediterranean. British possession of Crete provided protected naval harbors and threatened the German held Romanian oilfields. For the Germans, Crete allowed air operations to be conducted against British forces in North Africa and secured the southern flank for the invasion of the Soviet Union.[2] For the British, the defeat in Greece and the overall Mediterranean strategic setting shaped the operational environment for the Battle of Crete.

In April 1941, Wavell appointed Major-General Bernard Cyril Freyberg VC (1889 – 1963), to command all British[3] troops defending Crete. Freyberg was born in the United Kingdom, but raised in Wellington, New Zealand, becoming a dentist before World War I. Freyberg was gazetted as a second lieutenant with the 6th Hauraki Regiment in 1911, but could not secure a commission with the New Zealand Staff Corps. Freyberg was traveling overseas in 1914 when war was declared. At the time, Freyberg was in Mexico, reportedly fighting for "Pancho" Villa in the Civil War,[4] at which time he made his way to London to offer his services to England. Freyberg's World War I record is impressive:

> Freyberg secured a commission in the newly formed Royal Naval Division's Hood Battalion. . . . He was gazetted as a temporary lieutenant in the Royal Naval Volunteer Reserve, and given command of a company. Relishing the opportunity presented by the war ('I am in this with all my heart'), he took part in the brief, unsuccessful attempt to defend Antwerp in October 1914. Early in the Gallipoli campaign in 1915, he won a DSO for swimming ashore and setting diversionary flares at Bulair (Bolayir). He was wounded at Helles, returning in June to become commander of the Hood Battalion. He was badly wounded again in July, and eventually left the peninsula when the division was evacuated in January 1916. Transferring to the British Army, Freyberg was posted to the Queen's Royal West Surrey Regiment, but remained seconded to the Royal Naval Division, with which he proceeded to France in May 1916. During the final stages of the first battle of the Somme, he so distinguished himself in the capture of Beaucourt village that he was awarded a VC; he was again severely wounded in this action and evacuated to Britain. Returning to the front in February 1917, he was two months later appointed to command a territorial brigade in the 58th Division – reputedly becoming the youngest general in the British Army. In September a shell exploding at his feet inflicted the worst of his many wounds. When he resumed duty in January 1918 he again commanded a brigade (in 29th Division), performing with distinction during the German offensive of March–April 1918. He won a bar to his DSO in September that year. Freyberg ended the war by leading a squadron to seize a bridge at Lessines, which was achieved one minute before the armistice came into effect and which earned him another DSO. He had been made a CMG in 1917, and was mentioned in dispatches no fewer than five times during the war.[5]

Between the wars, Freyberg held a number of staff and command appointments in the British Army and was promoted to major-general in 1934 at age 45. Due to health problems, Freyberg retired in 1937, but with the declaration of World War II returned to active duty. In October 1939, the Acting Prime Minister of New Zealand, Peter Fraser,[6] visited England to discuss with the British Prime Minister, Winston Churchill, possible commanders of New Zealand's military forces, as no suitable general officer existed within the New Zealand Army. After discussions with Churchill and other higher ranking military officials, Freyberg was selected to command the Second New Zealand Expeditionary Force (2NZEF)[7] and its fighting arm, the 2nd New Zealand Division (2nd NZ Div).[8] Freyberg commanded the 2nd NZ Div from its formation and training 1940, through the North Africa, Balkans, and Italian campaigns to the conclusion of the war, only relinquishing command due to injury or illness, or to command at corps level.

The Battle of Crete in May 1941 is a much contested and debated operation by military historians, seeking to define the causes of the German operational victory and the British defeat. The battle affords a significant ease of study. It occurred over a relatively short timeframe and was limited to a small geographical area; the opposing forces were easily defined; and the outcome decisive. Whilst the tactical battle appears clear-cut, historians have continued to debate the circumstances that influenced the battle and the overall operational and strategic effect on both adversaries after the engagement. The declassification of intelligence in 1974, gained through breaking German wartime Enigma encryption codes (codenamed Ultra) has cast new light on intelligence sources and reopened debate about Freyberg's command of the battle.

The twelve days of battle for Crete was some of the bitterest fighting yet seen in the war. The *Official History of New Zealand in the Second World War* would later list British casualties as 1,751 killed, 1,738 wounded, and 12,254 prisoners of war.[9] Additional to these figures are some 2,000 Royal Navy personnel killed or wounded during the campaign, and over 5,000 Greek soldiers captured. German losses are difficult to establish. The Germans suffered almost 6,500 casualties of which 3,352 were killed or missing in action. Almost one-third of the Ju-52s used in the operation were damaged or destroyed.[10]

For the Germans, the campaign was a success but the cost high. Whilst they had achieved their strategic aim of securing their southeastern flank for Operation Barbarossa, they did not use Crete for any further offensive action in the Mediterranean, as Hitler turned his attention to the Soviet Union. Up to 50,000 soldiers were required to garrison the island after the battle to suppress the Greek resistance for the remainder of the war. In addition, the cost of the operation was not lost on the German hierarchy. "Even General Kurt Student[11] admitted that Crete had been 'the graveyard of the German paratroopers'. . . . Such an attrition rate was unacceptable to Hitler and after Operation Merkur,[12] he ordered that all future attacks involving the paratroopers of Germany should be part of an infantry attack."[13]

For Britain, the defeat was bitter. Churchill had looked to Crete to be the first decisive operational land victory of 1941 that would regain the offensive initiative in the Mediterranean. Immediately following the battle, the War Office in London held a series of inquiries into the failure of the operation. The New Zealand prime minister also sought assurances that Freyberg was the most capable officer to lead 2NZEF.

This focus of this thesis is to determine Freyberg's culpability for the loss of Crete. The research will investigate the operational environment that Freyberg faced, as Crete should not be examined in isolation from other operational and strategic influences evident in the Middle East and Mediterranean theater at the time. This will include the relationship between Freyberg and Wavell, the British and New Zealand Governments prior to and during the operation, and the priority of effort that Crete had within overall Allied strategy. The Battle of Crete was fought largely by the remnants of the failed Greece campaign and the existing garrison on the island, with air and sea support provided from outside of Freyberg's sphere of command. These considerations affected Freyberg's operational plan that will be examined in a later chapter.

The German *Luftwaffe* planned and conducted an audacious and daring campaign in Operation Merkur. This was the first predominantly airborne assault in history to capture an island. The German plan pitted air supremacy and the elite airborne troops of the *Luftwaffe* against the defenders. The British performance has been often cited as the reason for the fall of Crete, but was it simply a superior German plan that was better fought by the *Luftwaffe* operational and tactical commanders?

Since the declassification of Ultra, renewed debate has arisen about the forewarning and knowledge Freyberg had of the German invasion plan, gained from this source. This research will analyze the intelligence that Ultra provided and the method in which Freyberg was informed of the source, and his ability to utilize the information. At this stage of the war, intelligence services were in their infancy, and although decryption of German codes was an advantage, did it provide the operational commander with actionable intelligence on the battlefield that made a significant impact on the battle?

Freyberg's operational plan requires scrutiny. Was the plan sound, based upon the forces and information he had at the time? Very few communication assets were available to Freyberg during the battle and the dispersed location of his forces made direct leadership difficult. Therefore, his plan needed to be robust if he was out of contact with his subordinate units. Did Freyberg provide his subordinate commanders with sufficient direction (and resources) to carry out their missions? Did they comply with Freyberg's orders? The critical leadership decisions made by Freyberg and his subordinate commanders, and the German operational and tactical commanders will be examined including, when defeat was imminent, the conduct of the retreat from Crete.

The Allies enjoyed numerical superiority over the enemy, were in defended positions, and possessed credible intelligence and forewarning of the invasion plan. Yet they still lost the battle. Authors and historians have since identified a myriad of reasons why the battle was lost. These include poor equipment and communications, failed intelligence, uninspiring leadership, and a lack of cohesion between units. While Freyberg must, and did, accept the responsibility for the loss of the battle as the operational commander, was it due to a lack of operational command ability on his part, or circumstances beyond his control? Was General B.C. Freyberg VC culpable for the Allied loss at the Battle of Crete in 1941?

---

[1]General Sir Archibald Percival Wavell (1883–1950), son of a major-general and later promoted to field-marshal, was an intellectual as well as a soldier. He served with the Black Watch in World War I, losing an eye to a shell splinter. Wavell spent the interwar period in a number of training and command appointments including Palestine, ultimately promoted to General and appointed General Officer Commanding Middle East in July 1939. He came into conflict with Winston Churchill throughout much of his tenure, mostly regarding Churchill's interference in operations against initially the Italians, and later the Germans in North Africa and the Middle East. Churchill dismissed

Wavell from command in June 1941 following the battle of Crete, moving him to Commander-in-Chief India where he served out the war in this capacity and then as the Viceroy of India. Ian Beckett's chapter contained in John Keegan's book *Churchill's Generals* (New York: Quill William Morrow, 1991) provides further details on Wavell's career.

[2] Peter D. Antill, *Crete 1941, Germany's Lightening Airborne Assault* (Oxford, United Kingdom: Osprey Publishing, 2005), 8-12.

[3] The term "British Forces" includes British Army, Royal Marines, Royal Air Force, Cypriots, Palestinians, Australians, and New Zealanders who fought on Crete.

[4] This is hard to substantiate. A number of sources quote Freyberg as being in Mexico in different capacities including a guard for a film crew or working for a mining company, to being the officer in charge of Villa's transport. Other sources argue that Villa put a price on Freyberg's head, at which time he deserted and walked 300 miles in order to catch a boat to England.

[5] Ian McGibbon, *Freyberg, Bernard Cyril 1889-1963* (Dictionary of New Zealand Biography, updated 7 July 2005); available from http://www.dnzb.govt.nz/; Internet; accessed 16 September 2005.

[6] Peter Fraser (1884–1950) led the New Zealand Labour Party throughout the majority of World War II. Fraser used his influence as prime minister and good relationship with Churchill to support the war effort, including conscription and industrial support. Following the battles of Greece and Crete, and the Japanese attack on Pearl Harbour, Fraser faced significant pressure to bring 2NZEF home to fight in the Pacific, as the Australians had. Fraser convinced the War Cabinet that 2NZEF should remain in the Middle East as requested by Churchill, raising new units to fight in the Pacific theatre and developing closer defense ties with both Australia and the United States that would assist in the defense of New Zealand. Fraser won a further election in 1946, but after a long battle with illness died in 1950. Source: Tim Beaglehole, *Fraser, Peter 1884–1950.* (Dictionary of New Zealand Biography, updated 7 July 2005); available from http://www.dnzb.govt.nz/; Internet; accessed 17 September 2005.

[7] Paul Freyberg, *Bernard Freyberg VC: Soldier of Two Nations* (Kent, United Kingdom: Hodder and Stoughton, 1991), 200-201.

[8] These were distinctly different commands. The 2nd NZ Div was the fighting element of the New Zealand Army land forces in World War II. 2 NZEF, which Freyberg also commanded, comprised those units that were required to sustain 2nd NZ Div including reinforcements, training units, and specialist units such as hospitals, logistics, and base support units.

[9] Daniel M. Davin, *Official History of New Zealand in the Second World War, 1939-45 Crete* (Wellington, New Zealand: War History Branch, 1997), 486.

[10] Antill, 8-12.

[11] *Generaloberst* Kurt Arthur Benno Student (1890-1978) was initially commissioned as an infantry officer in World War I, however underwent pilot training and commanded a *Jagdstaffe* (fighter squadron) before being seriously wounded in 1917, and forced to convalesce for the remainder of the war. The limitations imposed by the Versailles Treaty on the development of motorized aircraft actually assisted Student, who was at the forefront of adapting gliders for military operations. Student also served as a *Reichswehr* infantry battalion commander and then, with the creation of the *Luftwaffe* under Göring in 1935, as the Instructor Flying Schools. In 1938, Student was given command of the 7th Air Division, and would continue to serve in airborne units for the remainder of World War II. Student was put on trial after the war for condoning reprisals against Cretan civilians, but was acquitted based largely upon the evidence of New Zealander Brigadier Inglis. Student was freed from captivity in 1948, and died in 1978. Student is looked upon as the forefather of paratrooper operations by many nations, and is widely revered for his innovative approaches, and fearless leadership. Source: Peter Antill, *Crete 1941: Germany's Lightening Airborne Assault* (Oxford, United Kingdom: Osprey, 2005), 20-21.

[12] Operation Merkur (Mercury) was the operational codename assigned to the 1941 German invasion of Crete.

[13] Christopher Ailsby, *Hitler's Sky Warriors, German Paratroopers in Action, 1939–1945* (Dulles, VA: Brassey's, 2000), 63.

CHAPTER 2

OPERATIONAL ENVIRONMENT

On 30 April 1941, twenty days before the first German paratroopers descended on Crete, General Wavell flew from Cairo to the island to meet with General Freyberg. The New Zealand commander was amidst regrouping New Zealand troops evacuated from Greece, prior to transportation to Alexandria, where he envisaged the 2NZEF would have time to reorganize, reequip and train before further operations. Wavell, however, had other plans. Wavell, on the recommendation of Winston Churchill, directed Freyberg to command all British forces on Crete (CREFORCE). Wavell also impressed on Freyberg that he considered an attack on Crete by the Germans to be imminent.[1]

The Battle of Crete that Freyberg and the British forces undertook in May 1941 occurred largely because of the greater strategic and operational environment and influences during the initial stages of the war. The command relationships between politicians and generals and the effect of campaigns and operations in North Africa, the Middle East and the Mediterranean (especially Greece) set the conditions for the Battle of Crete. Crete's strategic and operational importance within the region and British war plans; coupled with the influence, or lack thereof, of British naval and air forces all had secondary, if not direct effects on the Freyberg's conduct of the battle.

The strategic setting in late 1940 and early 1941 was a mixture of success and failure for the British, and in particular Middle East Command under Wavell. In the face of heavy Italian troop buildup in North Africa, Wavell initially sought to consolidate his forces (including Freyberg's 2NZEF) and undertake training in order to prepare a force capable of offensive operations. Concurrently, he secured Egypt as a logistical and future base of operations. This approach conflicted with Churchill who, by August 1940 with the defeat in France still fresh and the Battle of Britain raging overhead, was desperate for success.[2] Churchill continually pressed Wavell to go on the offensive and at times during 1940 threatened his dismissal. The relationship between Churchill and Wavell, whilst cordial and professional, continued to be strained, up until Wavell's dismissal as General Officer in Charge (GOC) Middle East Command after the Battle of Crete. Churchill thought Wavell too cautious and lacking drive, whereas Wavell found Churchill meddlesome in his command of the North Africa campaign.

Wavell launched Operation Compass against the Italians in December 1940 achieving a resounding and somewhat surprising success. In three months, British forces seized Cyrenaica and defeated an estimated ten Italian divisions, capturing over 130,000 prisoners for the loss of fewer than 2,000 British soldiers.[3] However, this was to be the limit of Wavell's success. In fairness, he faced an overwhelming theatre of operations that included by February 1941 more than just his battle against the Italians in Syria. Potential German offensives in Iraq, the Balkans, Cyprus, Malta, and Crete and the introduction of Rommel's *Deutsches Afrika Korps* in North Africa all required attention. The resources at Wavell's disposal were woefully inadequate to meet these contingencies.

Freyberg's 2NZEF was to feel the effect of the lack of British combat troops available in the North African campaign. Freyberg was determined that the 2nd NZ Div would concentrate in Egypt, train, and then be committed to battle as an entire division. This was in keeping with the mandate so carefully crafted by the New Zealand government when agreeing to Freyberg commanding the New Zealand forces in 1939.

The prime minister[4] directed Freyberg that the division be kept together and only committed to battle when Freyberg considered it to be at an effective trained and equipped state. This point was well known amongst the New Zealand soldiers who were confident that Freyberg would "protect them against the maneuvers of politicians and the vagaries of high level strategists."[5] However, senior British officers, much to Freyberg's chagrin, initially sought to piecemeal employ the division both in England and in North Africa.

The likelihood of invasion of Great Britain in September 1940 delayed 5th NZ Bde in England as part of a counterattack force.[6] While in the desert, Wavell pushed Freyberg and Lieutenant General Thomas Albert Blamey[7] to provide troops to garrison duties and support tasks to release British troops for Operation Compass. Wavell, as had British officers in the past, viewed all units under his command as a pool of British troops and not independent commands from the Dominion countries. This was somewhat arrogant, considering that most of troops fighting in North Africa were either from New Zealand, Australia, India, or North African countries and would bring Wavell and Freyberg into conflict during the upcoming Greek and Crete battles. Additionally, senior British officers viewed Freyberg at least initially, regardless of his appointment as the 2NZEF commander, to be a British officer (he was on the British Army List) who would defer to his British superiors over his New Zealand concerns if required. At times this did occur, when British commanders were able to impress on Freyberg the operational "necessity" of requests, which he could hardly deny. The delay in deploying 5th NZ Bde to Egypt from England due to the counterattack task, and Freyberg providing his Headquarters 2nd NZ Div signals unit as the headquarters element for Operation

Compass (at the detriment of his own command who were not part of the operation) are examples.

Freyberg's loyalty was torn between supporting his operational commander in the field and his political masters in New Zealand. His memorandum from the New Zealand government expressly made him the sole judge of the employment of 2NZEF with a direct responsibility and line of communication back to New Zealand without needing to consult with British commanders.[8] The command of 2NZEF and 2nd NZ Div, while appearing to have the same objective, were distinctly different in the field. The British saw 2nd NZ Div as a tactical unit to be employed as they saw fit and neglected to view the division within the greater overall context of being a national commitment from a small Commonwealth country. Blamey encountered the same problem with the Australian troops. The animosity between British and Dominion officers grew to a stage that preceding the Greek Campaign Wavell did not even consult Freyberg and Blamey in any of the operational planning undertaken by Middle East Command. This was despite these two countries providing the majority of the troops.[9]

In February 1941, Churchill looked to Middle East Command to provide troops to support diplomatic efforts in the Balkans in an effort to establish a Balkan front comprising Greece, Turkey, and Yugoslavia and to draw them into the war on the British side against Germany.[10] Neither Greece nor Turkey had until then committed to the war, and each had resisted British offers of assistance, especially troops on their soil lest they provoked the Germans to invade. Greece had repelled the Italian invasion two months previously, and only when it became obvious that Germany would invade Greece did the

Greek government request assistance from the British. Turkey also agreed to accept technical and equipment support.[11]

Having promised to support Greece in the event of German invasion, the political agreement of this alliance was not matched by the commitment of sufficient military resources. Greece had paid the price for defeating the Italian invasion. Despite their success, Greece did not possess the industrial power to replace material losses or keep its troops supplied.[12] The Greek government had identified that at least ten divisions additional to the available three Greek divisions would be required to defend against the German attack.[13] The lack of British divisions and the scant air resources available and allocated by Middle East Command would doom the Greek venture from the start, a fact not lost on the New Zealand Prime Minister. His first question to the United Kingdom Chiefs of Staff who planned and approved the Greek operation after the campaign was very pointed, "What were the grounds for believing that three divisions and an armoured brigade, plus the Greeks, could hold an unlimited number of German divisions, fully mechanized and armoured – plus the Italians?"[14]

Wavell directed the deployment of 2nd NZ Div to Greece on 17 February 1941. At this time, Freyberg still had yet to concentrate the division in one location and train as a unit, with 5th NZ Bde yet to arrive from England. The 2nd NZ Div formed part of an expeditionary force ("W Force") under General Sir Harry Maitland Wilson,[15] along with Blamey's 6th and 7th Aust Divs, a Polish brigade, and a British armored brigade. Middle East Command did not consult Blamey and Freyberg in the planning of the Greek operation. If they had been, it is likely they would have had misgivings about the commitment in what was becoming apparent as a forlorn hope.

Additionally, Wavell had miscalculated his strength in the desert to Churchill. Although not enamored with the Greek campaign as it took resources away from his North Africa operations, Wavell assured Churchill that by committing the expeditionary force to Greece, he retained a secure flank in North Africa, thus protecting Egypt. This was soon contradicted when Rommel easily defeated British forces at Benghazi, destroying much of the only remaining British armored division, and forced Wavell to cancel the deployment of 7th Aust Div and the Polish brigade to Greece. Additionally, resources, most notably air support, that were designated to support the Greek (and later Crete) campaigns, had to be reassigned to support the defense against Rommel.[16]

Wavell was not entirely honest either with Freyberg, assuring him that the British government had attained permission for 2nd NZ Div to be committed to the Greek campaign. By the time Fraser was fully appraised of the operational situation by Freyberg along with his misgivings about the chance of success of the operation, 2nd NZ Div had been committed to the campaign and had begun deploying to Greece. This had a secondary effect of committing Freyberg and 2nd NZ Div to the Battle of Crete, regardless of how either Freyberg or Fraser saw the employment of the division at the completion of the Greek campaign.

The tension between the generals and the politicians would continue to be evident later on during the Battle of Crete and the subsequent inquiries after it. Fraser, at the time of the battle was visiting in Egypt, and added his political weight to Freyberg's continued requests for additional resources. Freyberg's direct command responsibility to the New Zealand Government for 2NZEF matters allowed him to request support on behalf of the whole of CREFORCE, knowing that Fraser would take matters up with Churchill.

Although not bypassing Wavell (all requests to Fraser were also made to Middle East Command), the dual command chain caused understandable stress. Fraser's lobbying of both Wavell and Churchill to release aircraft to support CREFORCE and later to ensure that sufficient shipping was provided for the evacuation caused significant tension between the two prime ministers and their generals. While the political and military relationships that would result in Freyberg assuming command on Crete were being played out in late 1940 and early 1941 leading up to the Greek campaign, very little activity was happening on the island of Crete itself.

The importance of Crete strategically for both British and German forces was linked geographically to Greece (see appendix A). Germany, by invading Greece and Yugoslavia in order to secure their southern flank for Operation Barbarossa, was compelled to include Crete in their battle plans. If the British retained Crete, their sea and air power would be in a position to strike at operations in the Balkans, especially in Yugoslavia and Greece. Although at the extreme range of British bombers, they could also attack the Ploesti oilfields in Romania, the oil source needed for German industry. Crete provided a secure naval refueling base from which the British fleet could continue to dominate the eastern and greater Mediterranean, and in particular, defend the sea approaches to Malta. Crete, in German hands threatened British operations in North Africa and placed long-range bombers in a position to support Rommel in Libya and threaten British forces in Egypt, particularly if land operations were to be conducted as far east as the Suez Canal.

The geographical location and topography of Crete was distinctly against the defender, when considered in the context of this battle. Defending against an attack from the north (Greece or the Balkan region), the British defenders were automatically geographically isolated. The main towns and airfields of Máleme, Retimo and Heráklion, and the port at Suda Bay were all on the northern coast closest to the enemy (see appendix B). Of the airfields, only Heráklion was a permanent field, constructed using concrete. The remaining fields were temporarily established when the RAF began flying sorties in support of the Greek operation. The enemy was able to mass airpower from the southern air bases of Corinth, Eleusis, and Phalison on mainland Greece, and the short distance to Crete allowed for a long loiter time over the target and a quick turnaround for rearming, refueling, or reloading of troops and supplies. Conversely, air support for the defenders of Crete, if not from the island itself, had to come from North Africa almost 500 miles away, a distance that was at the extreme range of British air capability requiring the use of long-range Blenheim bombers. With no port on the southern side of the island, the position of Suda Bay on the northern coast also channeled sea resupply and naval operations into the Aegean Sea between the Greek mainland and Crete, forcing shipping into range of enemy air attack.[17] Freyberg himself said, "had it been possible to spin Crete round the story of the defense would probably have been the story of a successful siege."[18]

On the island, the only trafficable road ran along the northern coast from Máleme, through Canea and Retimo to Heráklion. This single coastal road was the resupply route during the battle and the only road along which reserves or reinforcements could deploy. This road of substandard construction additionally contained numerous bridges of various states of repair. Interdiction of this road either with ground forces, cratering or with air strikes would isolate the defenders in each of the towns until the route could be re-established. The road south from Canea to Sphakia was little more than a dirt track and was not suitable for movement of heavy equipment or vehicles like tanks and artillery pieces. This topography had a big impact on the conduct of the battle, from both the air and naval perspective to support Freyberg and the ground forces in the defense of Crete.

The strategic importance of Crete was not lost on Churchill especially as a naval foothold to be retained to protect Malta and Egypt while securing the flow of British oil and resources from the Persian Gulf through the Suez Canal. After the Italian Army attacked Greece on 28 October 1940, Churchill directed Wavell to fortify Suda Bay as a port facility and to prepare airbases on Crete.[19] The buildup of defenses at Suda Bay and Crete over the next six months was minimal, as Wavell had to balance Crete within the requirements of other operations. Crete itself was not seen as a likely battlefield by either Churchill or Wavell until April 1941. Churchill informed Wavell, "victory in Libya had priority over evacuation from Greece and that Crete will at first only be a receptacle of whatever we can get there from Greece. Its fuller defense must be organized later."[20] Tanks, antiaircraft and field guns, communications equipment and supplies that Freyberg was desperately short of during the battle, were required elsewhere.[21]

The situation was no better on Crete itself, where a succession of British officers were responsible for developing the defense of the island. No less than five officers commanded the British forces on Crete in the six months leading to Freyberg's assumption of command.[22] No coherent defense plan appeared until Marine Major-General Eric Weston[23] assumed command in late March 1941, and conducted a detailed reconnaissance of the defense of the island, which formed the basis for Freyberg's own appreciation. Road, airfield and port improvements should have been undertaken utilizing the Cretan population and the 15,000 Italian prisoners of war on the island including improving the route from Sphakia on the southern coast to the capital in Canea. This would have increased the mobility of the British garrison, and assisted in a coordinated defense plan for the island, as would the construction of airfields on the southern side of the island. Weston realized this in his appreciation completed at the same time British forces were withdrawing from the front lines in Greece, but by the time he handed over to Freyberg, however, there was not enough time to effect any significant improvement to the garrison defenses or local infrastructure.[24]

Crete was not considered a likely battlefield until April 1941, and Wavell had committed the expeditionary force under Wilson to Greece. Crete at that time comprised the naval refueling station, and three substandard airfields from which to provide air support to the campaign on the Greek mainland and pressure German operations in the Balkans. The lateness of the realization by Wavell, and indeed Churchill, that Crete would have to be defended contributed to the lack of preparation of the island defenses. Weston, commanding the Mobile Naval Base Defense Organization (MNBDO) capable of providing coastal, antiaircraft, field artillery and some infantry, was deficient three quarters of his force that were reassigned in Alexandria and the majority of its equipment, due to an administrative mix-up, remained in Palestine upon deployment. As it was, Weston was only able to deploy 2,200 of his command to Crete and minimal equipment when he assumed command.[25] Additionally, the MNBDO force was designed to defend naval installations from static locations. It was not trained as an infantry force capable of conducting coordinated ground maneuver such as a counterattack to seize terrain or defeat an enemy force.[26]

Greek armed forces on Crete prior to the battle were minimal. The Cretan V Division deployed as part of the Greek Royal Hellenic Army to repel the Italian invasion in 1940. This deployment occurred largely through Wavell and politicians in London convincing the Greek Government in October 1940 that by occupying Crete as a naval and air staging base, the British forces would assume responsibility for the defense of the island. In a somewhat cruel twist of fate, the troops best suited to the defense of the island would not be available for the battle. The Cretan V Division, along with most of the Hellenic Army, were cut off on the Albanian front after the Germans' lightning advance through Greece and Yugoslavia, and forced to surrender. Remaining on the island were approximately 4,000 Cretans not considered suitable for earlier deployment of which only one in five possessed a weapon.[27] Many of these civilians would later, under Freyberg's instigation, be formed into quasi home-guard battalions, lightly armed and equipped, yet would fight with great valor against both the German invasion and subsequent occupation.

The lack of equipment and supplies buildup on Crete prior to the Greek campaign commencing had an adverse effect on all three services from late March 1941 onwards when Weston and Wavell attempted to overcome the equipment and supplies shortfall. British air support from Crete or North Africa gained the attention of the *Luftwaffe* which commenced air attacks on Máleme, Heráklion and Retimo, and interdiction of British shipping bringing supplies for the garrison from Egypt. By mid-May 1941, eight of fifteen supply ships lay destroyed in Suda Bay, and only 3,000 tons of the anticipated 27,000 tons needed for the garrison were landed.[28] The equipment carried on these vessels was that identified by Freyberg upon assumption of command to augment or replace equipment lost during the withdrawal from Greece. While these activities were occurring in the operational environment outside of Freyberg's control, his 2nd NZ Div was committed to a campaign that would ultimately lead to their deployment to Crete and subsequently, the battle to defend it.

When ordered by Wavell to deploy to Greece on 17 February 1941, Freyberg finally was able to consolidate 2nd NZ Div as a complete formation with 5th NZ Bde arriving from England on 3 March 1941. 2nd NZ Div deployed as part of the Australia New Zealand Army Corps (ANZAC) under command of Australian General Blamey along with 6th Aust Div. On 5 April 1941, the corps deployed to the area of the Aliakmon River forming a defensive line in depth to the Greek Army that was forward.[29] The German Army advanced rapidly south from Yugoslavia under the cover of overwhelming air supremacy. This succeeded in forcing isolated Greek forces forward the ANZAC troops to withdraw and subsequently all British troops became in danger of being cut-off. Freyberg wrote, "If we had been forced to stay and fight on the Aliakmon Line, we should all have been rounded up in the first phase of the campaign."[30]

For the next two weeks, Freyberg and 2nd NZ Div fought a number of brigade and division delaying battles, trading ground for time against the German forces that had succeeded in defeating the majority of the Greek army and were now engaged in isolating the ANZAC forces. Freyberg demonstrated his ability to orchestrate a complex withdrawal, often delaying the enemy for significant periods and then retreating under the cover of darkness. The New Zealand troops faced continual air attack and had little armor to counter the German advance. With the prospect of the retreat turning into a rout, Freyberg demonstrated his coolness under fire and forward command style moving from brigade to brigade to coordinate movement and influence the battle. Freyberg could probably be considered lucky to have made it to Crete at all, with nine of his personal staff cars destroyed whilst moving around the battlefield.[31] Whilst New Zealand and Australian troops were engaged in slowing the German advance, politically however, the battle was ending. On 21 April 1941, the Greek government surrendered, and evacuation of British troops ordered. Freyberg discussed the situation with his subordinate commanders and, on order from Middle East Command, directed the destruction of all equipment less that which could be carried from Greece by hand. Insufficient time and available shipping prevented the force from withdrawing any heavier equipment as well as troops.

On 28 April 1941, the Royal Navy evacuated the last British troops from Greece leaving behind artillery, antiaircraft guns, armored vehicles, and stores unable to be withdrawn. The guns of nine field and medium regiments, three antitank regiments, numerous antiaircraft batteries, and over 8,000 wheeled and tracked vehicles would have been invaluable in the defense of Crete. 16,000 British and Commonwealth soldiers of the original 62,000 deployed to Greece were killed, wounded or taken prisoner.[32] Of those captured 2,000 were 2nd NZ Div reinforcements captured at Kalamata. Freyberg was among the last of the British forces to leave on 28 April 1941, having earlier ignored orders for him to leave on 23 April 1941. For the last week, he commanded the withdrawal and evacuation after the GOC General Wilson departed three days earlier. Freyberg was, by this stage, frustrated and highly critical at the lack of strategic planning for the Greek campaign. The evacuation, although always likely given the overwhelming superiority of the German forces committed to the campaign, was not planned early enough or in sufficient detail to remove equipment or stores that would be needed to establish the next defense in the Mediterranean. At one stage during the withdrawal, lacking any coherent direction from Wilson or the staff of W Force, Freyberg had to drive to Athens and direct coordinating instructions for the withdrawal of the his New Zealand and Blamey's Australian divisions.[33] Freyberg's account sums up his feelings heading to Suda Bay, Crete on 28 April 1941, "The ill-fated Greek adventure was over. The grim battle for Crete was about to begin."[34]

The rapid evacuation from Greece and subsequent decision to defend Crete placed Freyberg in an unenviable position, firstly as commander 2nd NZ Div, and then as the overall operational commander. As Freyberg was being named commander of CREFORCE, the 6th NZ Bde and HQ 2nd NZ Div were leaving Suda Bay for Alexandria to reconstitute at the 2NZEF base camp in Egypt. The departure of this convoy directed by Middle East Command Movement Control,[35] denied Freyberg much needed communications equipment and headquarters staff firstly to plan the upcoming battle, and to provide command and control during it. Freyberg was forced to constitute an ad-hoc staff from what remained of the 2nd NZ Div, and staff that Weston released from the MNBDO. Weston was not forthcoming with much support to CREFORCE headquarters, somewhat pettily believing he should have been named overall commander rather than Freyberg, retaining the MNBDO staff and equipment for his appointment as commander of the Suda Bay area.[36] Freyberg would later write:

> I did not know the true state of disorganization until I went to Crete Headquarters. . . . I had to start by taking men from units to make the headquarters staff, and although they tried hard, they were not in the accepted term a staff. One of the greatest mistakes in the evacuation from Greece was the failure to evacuate from Greece to Crete a headquarters staff of which there were at least four.[37]

The troops available to Freyberg ranged from the original Garrison force; under-resourced and untested in battle, and evacuees from the Greek campaign; either as complete units or stragglers. Many of these men were still recovering from the shock of defeat in Greece, and although battle-hardened, had low morale. The effect of fighting the Germans with their superior equipment and air force, coupled with the fact that they were at that stage of the war unbeaten as a ground force, played on the minds of the Commonwealth troops. Beaten back mostly by airpower, some units had not contacted the enemy directly on Greece. While defeated in Greece, most wanted to engage the enemy in ground battle, rather then constantly seeking cover from air attack.[38] Most units had insufficient heavy weapons or equipment, which was abandoned or destroyed during the evacuation. 2nd NZ Div was Freyberg's main combat unit available, although they were under-strength due to 6th NZ Bde and HQ, 2nd NZ Div departure to Egypt. The Australian 19th Bde Group, and the British 14th Bde made up the other available formed combat units. On paper, the allied force of 30,000 British and 11,000 Greek troops[39] appears a significant sized fighting formation; however this figure is somewhat misleading. Freyberg, during the first week of May 1941, petitioned both Fraser and Middle East Command to evacuate as many noncombatants as possible as his command included 10,000 British and 10,000 Greek troops without weapons, 800 Greek aviators without aeroplanes and 15,000 Italian prisoners of war.[40]

Added to Freyberg's growing dependency on Crete was his responsibility to protect the King of Greece, several members of the Royal Family and other Greek politicians, recently evacuated from the Athens. Although Freyberg argued they should have been evacuated immediately from the island given the impending attack and the adverse effect that would be felt by the Greek people should they be captured or killed, British higher commands and politicians felt that the presence of the King would strengthen Greek resolve against the Germans. Freyberg's 21 May 1941 reply to the Foreign Office signal stating, "do not consider present situation necessitates evacuation either of Royal Party or Ambassador's party,"[41] which was received *after* the invasion commenced highlights the additional burden placed upon him and CREFORCE:

> This place is not fit for important people. The King and Prime Minister were yesterday nearly taken prisoner when fifty parachute troops landed within 500 yards of their house in the hills. I learned of their escape only from a feint signal picked up last night. With their New Zealand escort, which I can ill afford to be without, the party will be on the south coast . . . now out of touch with us even by wireless. The Minister left at 3 o'clock this morning to join the Royal party if possible. They have been bombed all day, and the consul had actually to be dug out.[42]

While it was the right of the Greek King to remain on the island as long as he saw necessary to organize the defense of his own country, for Freyberg this was an additional burden and responsibility. Initially, what few Greek soldiers there were on the island were under local command with the King present on the island. All Greek soldiers were eventually placed under Freyberg's command however he was required to be cognizant of the Kings wishes when considering the employment of the rapidly organized Greek units. As Crete was not self-sustaining in peacetime, Freyberg also assumed the responsibility of ensuring the 400,000 citizens of the island had sufficient food to survive. The growing dependency on the island (civilian and military) would rely on the maintenance of the sea-lanes during the battle to ensure this. Supplying the civilian population as well as the military garrison was an additional factor and limitation for both Freyberg and Cunningham in the conduct of the defense of the island.[43]

While not short of personnel, CREFORCE was critically short of equipment. Cruiser Mk1 tanks were the only armor available and there was a significant shortage of motor transport with which to conduct resupply or form mobile reserves. Approximately eighty-five artillery pieces that either were withdrawn from Greece or formed part of the original island garrison were his only indirect fire support available. Many of these pieces were captured guns from the earlier Italian invasion of the mainland and lacked sights. Freyberg's critical equipment deficiency in hindsight would prove to be the lack of reliable communications equipment. There were few wireless sets available within CREFORCE, a fact exacerbated by Freyberg's own 2nd NZ Div headquarters having deployed to Egypt. The tactical difficulties of wide dispersion of troops to defend against the German invasion and lack of roads connecting the allied forces were compounded by the communications deficiencies. Freyberg's tactical and operational awareness during the battle would be constrained by what little wireless communications were available and what telephone lines remained intact between HQ CREFORCE and his subordinate units. In an attempt to ensure communications to CREFORCE, subordinate formations centralized the radios of their units, often leaving the battalions with few radio sets. 18th Bn was typical of most units; possessing only one set connecting the battalion headquarters to 4th NZ Bde; and no internal communications other than runners.[44]

Freyberg's initial reconnaissance of Crete confirmed that the island was not defendable without the full support of the Royal Navy and the RAF, the Navy to defeat a seaborne attack, and the RAF to support land and sea operations. Freyberg, whilst named as the operational commander did not carry the authority that this title of this position assumes. Freyberg, as the land commander, had no direct command authority over any of the air or naval forces during the battle as this was retained by single services, and was reliant on Wavell's ability to direct resources to Crete without diluting support to the operations in Iraq, Syria and North Africa. Wavell had briefed Freyberg that support from both Services would be limited but he would provide what he could. Air support available on Crete at the beginning of May 1941 was limited to six Hurricanes and seventeen obsolete aircraft operating from Máleme and Heráklion.[45] Freyberg asked that additional two squadrons be allocated from Royal Air Force Middle East to the defense of Crete to deny enemy air superiority and to assist with counterattacks. When this request was denied Freyberg was faced with overwhelming inferiority of air resources, compounded when the *Luftwaffe* commenced bombing and strafing of the island. Despite the pilots of the RAF continuing to operate from Crete regardless of appalling losses of equipment and aviators, Freyberg sought to prevent their total destruction prior to the invasion and ordered their evacuation to North Africa on 19 May 1941.

The overwhelming air superiority possessed by Germany in the Balkans and Mediterranean at the time of the Battle of Crete has lent credence to the argument by some historians that the lack of Allied air support was the main factor resulting in CREFORCE failing to hold the island. The impact on the tactical battle will be examined in further chapters, but an overview of the operational air environment around Crete is required. Stopping Rommel's advance through Africa occupied the majority of the RAF assets stationed on that continent. Sorties from Crete against German air bases in Greece were opposed by fighters and heavy antiaircraft fire. Therefore, striking at the *Luftwaffe* glider and transport plane buildup prior to the airborne invasion (later touted by some analysts as the best chance to defeat the attack) would have proved only possible if willing to accept heavy losses that the RAF could scarcely afford. At the time of the battle, Air Chief Marshal Sir Arthur Longmore, CinC RAF Middle East, responsible for all air operations Egypt, Libya, Iraq, Cyprus, and Crete had only a mix of ninety twin-engine aircraft and forty-three Hurricane fighters to conduct all air missions in the theater and therefore could not conduct such an operation.[46]

The scarcity of air resources affected the Royal Navy in the Battle of Crete as much as the land forces. Admiral Sir Andrew Cunningham, CinC Royal Navy Mediterranean had utilized Suda Bay as a refueling and rearming base after the fleet withdrew from Malta in 1940 owing to its close proximity to Italian air bases in Sicily. Occupation of air bases in southern Greece forced the fleet to move again, this time to Alexandria although this placed Cunningham in a difficult situation. He could not replenish Crete from Alexandria or provide naval gunfire support without drawing the attention of the *Luftwaffe*, especially if he wanted to conduct operations close to Crete by day. Cunningham enjoyed dominance of the Mediterranean against the German and Italian navies; however without air fighter support was vulnerable to air attack.

To his and the Royal Navy's credit, Cunningham supported the Army in early 1941 through the two difficult retrograde operations of Greece and Crete, with limited air support. The Royal Navy sustained heavy ship and personnel losses prior to and during the Battle of Crete preventing the total isolation of the island. This included sustaining severe damage to the only aircraft carrier, HMS *Formidable*, supporting Crete, which would require extensive repairs and leave the fleet even more vulnerable to air attack for the next three months after the battle. Freyberg would later remark, "Of the three

Services, the Navy made the fewest mistakes. . . . There were weak links in our chain of defense of Crete, but the Navy was not one of them."[47]

This then, is the environment that Freyberg was faced with as he commenced planning for the defense of Crete. Strategically, with British forces in retreat throughout much of the North African and Mediterranean theaters, Wavell was unable to allocate Freyberg any priority of effort for resources including air and equipment support. Crete had been badly neglected in the lead up to the battle despite its strategic importance in Mediterranean, Balkan and North African strategy. The island did not lend itself geographically to defense if attacked from the north and had little in the way of defensive preparation or improvement to existing infrastructure conducted by preceding commanders.

Freyberg had to consider not only his own command relationship with Wavell as his immediate military superior and the lack of unity of command for the operation between the services, but also the relationships at the political level with Fraser and Churchill that grew more and more strained. This became increasingly so, as Freyberg (through Fraser) sought resources with which to conduct the battle, but also to preserve the 2nd NZ Div from disintegration as a national fighting force. The commitment of Freyberg and the 2nd NZ Div to the ill-fated Greek campaign to satisfy political necessity led indirectly to his assumption of command of CREFORCE. The withdrawal and evacuation from Greece to Crete, less nearly all the force's heavy equipment including tanks, artillery and antiaircraft guns, further degraded the capacity of the troops fighting on Crete. The interdiction of naval and air operations in the theater leading to the battle shaped Freyberg's operational plan. The loss of much needed supplies and equipment to air attacks on Royal Naval shipping, and the lack of air support available to him to interdict German fighter, bomber and transport sorties left CREFORCE isolated from support other than what the Royal Navy could force through under attack from the German *Luftwaffe*.

Faced with the environment outlined in this chapter, Freyberg was somewhat hesitant to assume command of CREFORCE, and after his appreciation of the defenses of the island sent signals to both the New Zealand Government, and the Middle East Command, outlining his concerns about the lack of air support and the state of the troops and equipment. By this stage however, Churchill was determined that the island be 'stubbornly defended' and was a 'fine opportunity for killing airborne troops.'[48] He saw this as an ideal opportunity to dent the growing mystique and legend that was developing around the elite *Luftwaffe* airborne troops. Churchill's 'defend at all costs' approach to Crete intensified after his epic 'blood, toil, tears and sweat' speech made in the House of Commons on 13 May 1941. Freyberg, although still harboring doubts about his ability to defend the island with the resources he had available, was positive in the lead up to battle. Provided the Navy could defeat any seaborne attack on the island, he felt that the troops could give a good account of themselves in dealing with any airborne troops that attacked.[49] He could not foresee however, the overwhelming air superiority of the German *Luftwaffe* that was about to be launched against him.

---

[1]Paul Freyberg, *Bernard Freyberg VC: Soldier of Two Nations* (Kent, United Kingdom: Hodder and Stoughton, 1991), 266.

[2]John Keegan, *Churchill's Generals* (London, United Kingdom: Weidenfeld and Nicholson, 1991), 75.

³Harold E. Raugh Jr., *Wavell in the Middle East, 1939-1941* (London, United Kingdom: Brassey's (UK), 1993), 130.

⁴Michael Joseph Savage was the Prime Minister of New Zealand in January 1940 when the mandate to Freyberg was written. Savage was terminally ill by this stage with cancer, and most of the diplomatic effort between New Zealand and Great Britain immediately prior to, and in the early stages of the war fell to Peter Fraser as the Deputy Prime Minister. Fraser became the Prime Minister when Savage died on 27 March 1940.

⁵Ian Stewart, *The Struggle for Crete: 20 May-1 June 1941, A Story of Lost Opportunity* (London, United Kingdom: Oxford University Press, 1966), 50.

⁶Freyberg, 231.

⁷Lieutenant General (later Field Marshal) Sir Thomas Blamey (1884–1951) commanded firstly 6th Aust Div at the onset of the war, then the 1st Aust Corps and in North Africa and Greece. Blamey would be Australia's top soldier throughout the war, and a controversial one. In the desert, he fought to keep the Australian Corps together as a single fighting unit and only committed upon the approval of the Australian government, much the same as Freyberg did for the New Zealand Division. He commanded all the Australian forces in the Pacific against the Japanese, but lost favor with many of his subordinates for not standing up to MacArthur when he questioned the fighting spirit of the Australian soldiers. Promoted to Field Marshal on his deathbed, he is the only Australian soldier to reach this rank. Further details are contained within David Horner's biography, *Blamey: the Commander-in-Chief*, (Sydney, Australia: Allen and Unwin, 1998).

⁸War History Branch New Zealand, *Official History of New Zealand in the Second World War, 1939-45, Documents Relating to New Zealand's Participation in the Second World War1939-45, Vol 1* (Wellington, New Zealand: War History Branch Department of Internal Affairs, 1949), 31-32.

⁹Freyberg, 236.

¹⁰John Crawford, *Kia Kaha: New Zealand in the Second World War* (Oxford, United Kingdom: Oxford University Press, 2000), 20.

¹¹Winston S. Churchill, *The Second World War, Volume 3, The Grand Alliance* (Boston: Houghton Mifflin Company, 1950), 64-66.

¹²Francis de Guingand, *Operation Victory* (New York: Charles Scribner's Sons, 1947), 51.

¹³Crawford, 25.

[14] W. G. McClymont, *Official History of New Zealand in the Second World War, 1939-45, To Greece* (Wellington, New Zealand: War History Branch Department of Internal Affairs, 1959), 491.

[15] General (later Field Marshal) Sir Henry Maitland Wilson (1881–1964) served in both the Boer War and World War 1. He commanded British forces in Egypt prior to the Greek campaign and was appointed Commander-in-Chief Middle East after Montgomery's success against Rommel. Upon promotion to Field Marshal, he succeeded Eisenhower as the Supreme Allied Commander in the Mediterranean in 1944.

[16] Freyberg, 249.

[17] de Guingand, 82.

[18] Daniel M. Davin, *Official History of New Zealand in the Second World War, 1939-45, Crete* (Wellington, New Zealand: War History Branch, Department of Internal Affairs, 1953), 41.

[19] Churchill, 269.

[20] Ronald Lewin, *The Chief: Field Marshall Lord Wavell, Commander-in-Chief and Viceroy, 1939-1947* (New York: Farrar Strous Giroux, 1980), 116.

[21] Ibid., 131.

[22] Two officers, Major-General Gambier-Parry and Brigadier-General Galloway, had to depart suddenly for command appointments during this period, Parry to command 2nd Armored Division in Africa, and Galloway to Greece. This was typical of the fluid nature and high tempo of operations in the theatre at the time.

[23] Major-General (later Lieutenant-General) Eric Culpeper Weston (1888–1950) of the Royal Marines commanded the Mobile Naval Base Defense Organization (MNBDO) during the war. Freyberg, who assumed command of Crete from Weston, would hand back command of the island to him on the night of 30 May 1941 when he was ordered to evacuate to Egypt. Weston himself was evacuated by the last flying boat from Crete on the night of 31 May 1941.

[24] Lewin, 131-132; and de Guingand, 86.

[25] Davin, 6.

[26] Sir John White, interviewed by Sergeant Brenton Beach, 8 March 2004, interview 7a, transcript, Queen Elizabeth II Army Memorial Museum Veterans Oral History Project, Waiouru, New Zealand. Sir John White served as Freyberg's Personal Assistant on Crete in HQ CREFORCE.

[27] Antony Beevor, *Crete: The Battle and the Resistance* (London, United Kingdom: John Murray Ltd., 1991), 55.

[28] Christopher Shores, Brian Cull, and Nicola Malizia, *Air War for Yugoslavia, Greece and Crete* (London, United Kingdom: Grub Street, 1987), 328; and Stewart, 97.

[29] Freyberg, 238.

[30] Ibid., 250.

[31] Laurie Barber and John Tonkin-Covell, *Freyberg: Churchill's Salamander* (London, United Kingdom: Century Hutchinson Ltd., 1990), 5.

[32] Ibid., 244 and 260.

[33] Sir John White, interview 7b.

[34] Ibid., 262.

[35] Sir John White, interview 7a.

[36] Callum MacDonald, *The Lost Battle: Crete 1941* (New York: The Free Press, 1993), 145.

[37] Stewart, 52.

[38] Haddon Donald, interviewed by Sergeant Brenton Beach, 19 September 2001, interview 3b, transcript, Queen Elizabeth II Army Memorial Museum Veterans Oral History Project, Waiouru, New Zealand. Haddon Donald served as a platoon commander in 22nd Bn on Greece and Crete.

[39] Davin, 46.

[40] War History Branch New Zealand, 294-296.

[41] Freyberg, 293.

[42] Ibid., 293.

[43] Stewart, 93.

[44] William Denham Dawson, *Official History of New Zealand in the Second World War, 18 Battalion and Armoured Regiment* (Wellington, New Zealand: War History Branch, Department of Internal Affairs, 1953), 124.

[45] Freyberg, 273.

[46] Shores, Cull, and Malizia, 312.

[47]Freyberg, 296.

[48]Churchill, 269.

[49]War History Branch New Zealand, 404.

CHAPTER 3

OPERATION MERKUR

> We are few yet our blood is wild,
> Dread neither foe nor death.
> One thing we know – for Germany in need – we care
> We fight, we win, we die,
> To arms! To arms!
> There is no way back, no way back.
>
> German Paratrooper Song

History, traditionally, tends to look favorably on the victors. The Battle of Crete is a good example of an operation, however, where the failure of the British forces has been examined in far greater detail than the success of the German *Luftwaffe*. While many causes for British defeat have been identified and historians have apportioned blame as they see warranted, very few writers point to the successful planning and conduct of Operation Merkur by the staff, officers, and soldiers of the *Luftwaffe* as being the decisive factor. Rather, it was a British defeat, not a German success. Operation Merkur was the first solely airborne operation conducted in World War II, and therefore the planning and conduct of this new style of warfare had a definitive effect on the outcome of the battle. The operational and tactical decisions that were made by German commanders after the commencement of the airborne invasion will be discussed in a later chapter, where as this chapter will concentrate on the strategic and operational planning undertaken by the *Luftwaffe* in order to conduct the operation.

The failure of the *Luftwaffe* in the Battle of Britain to defeat the RAF by October 1940 did not lend itself to a potential German invasion of England (Operation Sealion) that summer. Hitler's plan to invade was premised upon setting favorable conditions including the crippling of the British military, especially the destruction of the RAF. With Operation Sealion effectively shelved for the foreseeable future, Hitler sought to attack Britain through the more indirect approach of attacking Britain's position in the Mediterranean and Middle East. This peripheral strategy, developed by *Generaloberst* Alfried Jodl,[1] was designed to cut England off from the remainder of the Empire, and deny her the rich flow of resources that traveled through the Suez and Mediterranean Sea areas.[2] Options examined by the High Command of the Armed Forces (OKW) under Führer Directive No. 18 included Gibraltar via Spain, Malta, Cyprus, Crete and the seizure of the Suez Canal and Egypt from Libyan bases.[3]

Key planning factors became quickly apparent to the OKW staff. Firstly, to seize Gibraltar, therefore dominating the Western Mediterranean, would require either General Fransico Franco[4] to bring Spain into the war on Germany's side, or at a minimum agree to German invasion forces transiting from France through Spain. Franco refused both, and the plan to invade Gibraltar was only seriously considered thereafter as a solely airborne option. Second, Germany was wary of the strength of the British Royal Navy Mediterranean Fleet which, originally based at Malta, now operated from Alexandria since Italy entered the war. The Navy's ability to interdict shipping and resupply lanes, and repel or influence a seaborne invasion force operating in the Mediterranean limited planning options.

Crete's strategic importance was realized by OKW, both as a means to protect the flank of any operation in the Balkans, and as a potential base from which to support operations in North Africa and the Suez Canal area. Initially in 1940, Hitler sought to secure this area by diplomacy, hoping that the neutrality (or support to Germany) of

Yugoslavia and Greece would provide him geographical flank protection to his planned operations in the Soviet Union, and resources of the Balkans upon which the German military depended. Although Hitler preferred Italy to remain out of the Balkans at that stage, when Benito Mussolini announced his intention to invade Greece, OKW pressed upon their Italian counterparts the need to synchronize this operation with those undertaken in North Africa. Additionally, when meeting with Mussolini in Florence on 28 October 1940, Hitler offered a division each of airborne and parachute troops with which to take the strategically important island of Crete as part of the invasion force.[5] Crete at that stage was largely undefended by British troops and consisted of only the naval garrison and no aircraft. Three days after Mussolini refused Hitler's offer of troops[6] and the Italian invasion of Greece began, Britain landed planes on Crete and began supporting operations in the Balkans.

By March 1941, Mussolini's failures in North Africa and the Balkans compelled Hitler to intervene. As early as December 1940, Hitler had been working on options for eventual military intervention in Greece and on 13 December 1940 issued Führer Directive No. 20 outlining Operation Marita, the invasion of Greece. This order was quickly followed, five days later, with Führer Directive No. 21, the planning guidance for Operation Barbarossa, the invasion of Soviet Union.[7] Hitler's focus had by this time clearly turned to Soviet Union, with planning guidance in Directive No. 20 directing that operations in the Balkans to be complete by 15 May 1941 in order to allow Barbarossa to commence. The Coup d'état in Yugoslavia overthrowing the government that just signed the Tripartite Pact with Germany in late March 1941, coupled with the continued buildup of British forces in Greece compelled Hitler to commence his Balkan operation. On 6

April 1941, Germany's 12th Army and 2nd Army invaded Yugoslavia and Greece. At the same time Hitler, wary of the drain on resources the Balkans campaign would have on his preparations for Barbarossa, postponed this operation until 22 June 1941.[8] On 15 April 1941, a week before capitulation of the Hellenic 1st Army and overall Greek surrender, the head of the *Luftwaffe Generalfeldmarschal* Hermann Göring[9] was presented with a plan for the seizure of Crete.

Crete was not the only objective considered for airborne operations by Göring and the staff at OKW in early 1941. Gibraltar still remained favored given its ability to block the Western Mediterranean, however was considered not able to be taken by a parachute descent alone and would require ground support and heavy artillery. Additionally the terrain did not provide sufficient glider landing areas or parachute drop zones, and the plan, effectively untenable by Franco's neutrality, was shelved in January 1941. Malta posed similar problems, being small and rocky with numerous obstacles to airborne and airlanding operations. Its small size would also allow defensive forces to quickly concentrate and oppose the airborne attack. Although the plan to invade Malta would remain an option through into mid-1942; the invasion of Greece by Germany made an airborne operation in the Eastern Mediterranean to seize either Crete or possibly Cyprus a more logical decision.[10]

The greatest proponent of airborne operations in the German military at this stage of the war, and operational commander that opposed Freyberg during the Battle of Crete was *Generaloberst* Kurt Student.[11] Student led the development of German airborne operations throughout the 1930s combining his experiences as an infantry officer and pilot in World War I and the inter-war period. As a flying instructor and member of the

Fliegerzentral (Central Flying Office) staff, Student traveled widely in the 1920s observing the rapid development of aircraft and its potential military application in other countries while Germany remained restricted in their own development of an air force by the Treaty of Versailles. This changed almost overnight when in January 1933 Hitler was sworn as the Chancellor of Germany and removed the restraints placed upon the Armed Forces for training, equipping, and recruiting. The establishment of the *Luftwaffe* sped the development of German aircraft design and development from 1935, requiring an experienced officer to command the experimental unit. Newly promoted to *Oberst* and commander of the unit, Student was responsible for everything from complete aircraft development to weapon systems to parachutes.[12] Student, impressing Göring with his industry and innovative approaches, was promoted to *Generalmajor* in 1938 and given command of the newly formed 7th *Flieger* Div. The *Flieger* Div combined the soldiers of the Army, and the transport aircraft of the *Luftwaffe* into a single unit.

Parachute operations were still in its infancy at this period although the possibility of dropping soldiers from aircraft behind or onto enemy lines had been touted as early as 1918 when Brigadier-General Billy Mitchell, commander of the U.S. Air Corps in France proposed dropping parachutists behind German lines at Metz. Assessed as an operation taking six months to train and equip, the idea was abandoned prior to the cessation of hostilities.[13] While some countries continued to develop parachuting as a means of survival for the pilot or to insert sabotage units behind enemy lines, it was the Soviet Union that first demonstrated in 1935 the feasibility of the airborne and airlanding attack, parachuting a regiment of 1000 men onto an objective and then immediately reinforcing by airlanding of 2500 troops including heavy weapons. The force then conducted a conventional infantry attack. Present at the demonstration were Herman Göring and Kurt Student from Germany, and Major-General Archibald Wavell from Britain. Wavell, while impressed with the demonstration, did not feel the lightly armed troops would be able to overcome ground troops in the defense especially if reinforced with tanks.[14]

Based on his observations of the Soviet trials, the development of the Junkers Ju52 transport aircraft and static-line silk chutes, Student and his staff conducted trials to develop their own tactics, techniques, and procedures while recruiting soldiers and officers to the division who showed leadership, determination and drive. All parachutists were volunteers, underwent rigorous selection testing and training, and formed what was to become a *corps d'élite*. Student overcame the problem of how to deploy heavier weapons and equipment by trialing and adopting the use of gliders, including the DFS 230 that would be used at Crete, which was towed by the Ju52 transport aircraft and could carry about 2,500 pounds.

The German annexation of the Sudetenland in September 1938 was to be the first test of the 7th *Flieger* Div, however a peaceful diplomatic resolution saw Student's troops restricted to a conducting a practice airlanding. 1938 did, however, see an evolution of airborne operations, with OKW designating the *Luftwaffe's* 7th *Flieger* Div as a purely parachute force, while the Army's 22nd *Luftlande* Div (although not trained to conduct parachute operations) became an airlanding force under operational control of the *Luftwaffe*. Student was however, still responsible for training some units of the Army in parachuting, and by the start of World War II, inter-service rivalry had started to develop amongst the Army and *Luftwaffe* staffs.[15]

The development of *Blitzkrieg* tactics within the German military, especially the employment of speed and shock of armor and airpower to overwhelm the enemy's command and control and strike deep into their rear areas, bypassing their combat units, was well suited to the evolving parachute doctrine. "Vertical envelopment" from the air by parachute could seize critical points and objectives, rapidly building up forces using airlanding before the enemy could regain the initiative, and either defeat them or fix them for later destruction by advancing armored forces. Shock and surprise were critical to demoralize the enemy who could no longer be assured of where the front lines were or direction of attack if facing an airborne force.[16]

Student and Göring actively campaigned for the 7th *Flieger* Div to be allocated a role in the invasion of Poland, after demonstrating to the OKW staff a massed parachute drop prior to the invasion. Placed in reserve, Student's troops would not be required, however, due to the overwhelming success of the *Panzer* invasion. When Hitler turned his attention to France and the Low Countries, he directed that full use was to be made of the airborne troops.[17] Student conducted two operations in support of the German invasion of the Low Countries in May 1940. Firstly, 7th *Flieger* Regt parachuted and landed by glider near and onto the Eban-Emael Fortress in Belgium, seizing it and a critical bridge that guarded the River Meuse. The force linked up with ground forces twenty-four hours later and sustained low casualties. Secondly, in an operation commanded personally by the newly promoted *Generalleutnant* Student, an ad-hoc airborne corps containing both the 7th *Flieger* Div and 22nd *Luftlande* Div, jumped and airlanded in Holland to seize key bridges over the Waal, Maas and Lower Rhine, and attempted to capture the Dutch royal family.[18] Despite missing landing zones in some areas and stiff opposition from the Dutch forces, Student achieved total surprise. Dutch High Command was overwhelmed with reports of paratroop drops all over the country, including dummies as deception, and was not able to mount a coordinated response. Reinforced by massive air support Student retained his objectives until linking up with advancing *Panzer* units. Student demonstrated decisiveness throughout this battle that was later evident at the Battle of Crete. At one stage when he possessed no reserve, he deployed the battalion guarding his only airfield capable of receiving resupply to reinforce a key bridge in his area and defeated the enemy attack, therefore securing a tactical victory.[19]

At The Hague, the operation was ultimately successful, but the casualties high. The paratroopers and airlanding force was met with stiff resistance from Dutch forces. Almost one-third of the force was killed or wounded and two-thirds of the transport aircraft lost. Although a tactical and operational success, the risks associated with this new form of warfare were exposed at this early stage.[20] For Student, the operation almost cost him his life. On 14 May 1940, when entering Rotterdam, he was shot in the head and had to be evacuated.[21]

The airborne operation in Holland provided the *Luftwaffe* with tactical and operational lessons, some of which would be implemented for the Battle of Crete, others which would be ignored. The operation was a success owing largely to the element of surprise, attainable due to being the first of its kind in history. Surprise coupled with boldness in planning and execution was critical for airborne operations. Success was attained by attacking limited objectives and linking up with ground forces within twenty-four hours. Airborne operations drew the enemy's attention away from ground operations and had potential as a diversionary tactic. Close coordination of bomber and fighter escort with both transporters and troops on the ground were difficult if communications were not sound, and air superiority proved essential prior to the airdrop and airlanding operations by isolating the battlefield surrounding objectives from reinforcement. Troops in the 22nd *Luftlande* Div required a greater level of training and coordination with the parachute troops, which would be achieved by permanently assigning them to the *Luftwaffe*.[22]

Student emerged from convalescence a *Generalleutnant* and commander of the now permanently established airborne corps, XI *Fliegerkorps* consisting 7th *Flieger* Div, 22nd *Luftlande* Div, a *Sturmregiment* capable of parachute and glider operations, and associated corps level combat support troops and equipment.[23] Owing to their success in Holland, the airborne troops had become a favorite of both Hitler and Göring, although they were not considered for the initial invasion of the Soviet Union in Operation Barbarossa. Inter-service rivalry pushed Göring to seek employment of the XI *Fliegerkorps,* and he looked to the Balkans theatre to demonstrate the prowess of the *Luftwaffe*, and regain favor after the earlier setbacks of the Battle of Britain. Göring saw the Balkans, especially the seizure of Crete as a stepping stone to further operations against North Africa and the Suez Canal, whereas Hitler, his eyes firmly fixed on the Soviet Union, viewed the Crete operation as the crowing glory of the Balkans campaign.[24]

Student's immediate superior, *Generaloberst* Alexander Löhr,[25] commander of *Luftflotte* IV briefed Göring on the possibility of German forces taking Crete in 15 April 1941. Student, met with Göring on 20 April 1941 and then Hitler on 21 April 1941 to brief them on an upcoming regimental level airborne operation to seize Corinth on the Greek mainland. At these meetings, he convinced both of them that the Crete operation could be conducted using airborne forces alone. Hitler, mindful of the impending Barbarossa campaign, agreed to the operation however imposed some limitations that hindered Student's planning and conduct of the battle. Firstly, the deployment of the 22nd *Luftlande* Div, which had been deployed to guard the Romanian oilfields at Ploesti against sabotage, to its assembly areas, was not to interfere with the concentration of troops for Barbarossa.[26] Second, once complete, the occupation of Crete (and Greece) Hitler envisaged being taken over by the Italians in order to maximize German forces available for Barbarossa, therefore the operation was to commence no later than 17 May 1941. Lastly, Hitler saw the Crete campaign as potential deception plan to the upcoming Operation Barbarossa that he was attempting to sell to Joseph Stalin as a feint. Hitler even tried to sell the Crete operation as a trial for a possible landing in Britain. Therefore operational security, much to Student's disgust given airborne operations reliance on the element of surprise, was lax during the planning for the Crete operation, especially above the *Luftflotte* IV level.

Hitler issued Führer Directive No. 28 on 25 April 1941 under the codename Operation Merkur. Command of the operation was delegated to Göring and the *Luftwaffe*, who in turn delegated the operation to Löhr and *Luftflotte* IV. The Army was directed to make "suitable reinforcements for the airborne troops, including a mixed armored detachment, which can be moved to Crete by sea."[27] This movement was to be controlled by the *Kriegsmarine* utilizing Italian resources. Student, named the operational commander by Löhr, initially sought to have VIII *Fliegerkorps*, responsible for providing the fighter cover and bombers to support the operation, also placed under his command along with his own XI *Fliegerkorps* as a means to overcome some of the command and control problems he had encountered in the Dutch operation. Löhr refused this, retaining control of all air assets within the Mediterranean. This was a sensible decision as it allowed him to coordinate not only the air effort against ground and air assets on Crete, but also to interdict the Royal Navy operating in the Mediterranean area. Additionally, it allowed him to mediate between his two corps commanders Student and *General der Flieger* Freiherr (Baron) von Richthofen[28] who had a strained but professional relationship. Headquartered in Poland, Richthofen was as ambitious as Student was, and viewed the operation a side-show to supporting Army Group Centre as they prepared for Operation Barbarossa.[29] A consummate professional however, neither his relationship with Student nor his personal view on Operation Merkur prevented Richthofen from providing overwhelming bomber and fighter escort support to the operation.

With the operation approved, Student had three weeks in which to plan and mount Operation Merkur. Student's first priority was to concentrate his force in Greece, owing to their dispersed locations in southern Germany from previous operations and training. By 10 May 1941, he had 7th *Flieger* Div and the *Sturmregiment* co-located and concentrated with VIII *Fliegerkorps* squadrons at airfields in southern Greece. 22nd *Luftlande* Div was unable to be released from its Ploesti security task in sufficient time to concentrate with the remainder of the corps; therefore the Army's 5th *Gebirg* (Mountain) Div commanded by *Generalmajor* Julius Ringel[30] was allocated to Student under operational control. Ringel's division had fought in Operation Marita and, although elite alpine troops, did not have any experience in airlanding operations. With Operation

Barbarossa troop movement and concentration causing additional delays, all forces allocated to Operation Merkur finally concentrated in Greece on 14 May 1941. This delay forced Student to postpone the commencement of the airdrop phase until 20 May 1941.[31]

Logistics also played a significant part on the preparation of the operation. XI *Fliegerkorps*' entire organic air transport assets had been withdrawn to Austria after the Corinth operation for refurbishment. It was testimony to the industry of the German war machine that they returned all of these aircraft within two weeks in time for the operation. However, the 520 Ju 52s of the XI *Fliegerkorps* were the only air transport assets available for the operation, and had to be used for both airlanding and parachute operations of 7th *Flieger* Div and 5th *Gebirg* Div as well as providing the logistical air link until seaborne forces arrived. Immediately this limitation directed the planning into phasing the operation based upon aircraft space rather than the massed shock effect that had previously been achieved when free of resource constraints.

The first truly operational level airborne assault conducted by the *Luftwaffe*, there was no ground linkup with Army units planned as had occurred in previous operations such as in Holland. Therefore the *Luftwaffe* was responsible for all planning. The German Army General Staff and *Kriegsmarine* were not involved in planning other than once the formal orders had been issued. The *Luftwaffe* did not possess a good record of operational planning, the failure of the Battle of Britain as an example, and used a system where planning was retained at the highest general officer level.[32] Their reluctance to involve subordinate staffs from other services restricted their planning process. This included a failed appreciation and poor reconnaissance of the enemy strengths and dispositions on Crete, a priority that a ground commander of Army background would likely have prioritized, and a flawed seaborne plan that was treated as little more than an afterthought to the air operation.

One of the greatest failings of Operation Merkur planning was the lack of credible intelligence gained prior to the operation including estimates of enemy strength and disposition. Given that paratroop commanders could not conduct ground reconnaissance ahead of their units; they could only rely on the information that was provided to them. No ground commanders conducted aerial reconnaissance prior to the operation; a lesson learnt that was identified by German commanders after the war. Therefore they did not have a great understanding of the terrain they were to encounter or the disposition of the enemy. Detailed reconnaissance had been conducted prior to the Dutch operation and well in advance combining information from numerous photo, reconnaissance, human intelligence and radio intercept sources. Given the short period of time to prepare and conduct the operation, Student was limited largely to what aerial photography could be provided from his own and Richthofen's reconnaissance squadrons.[33] The information proved to woefully inadequate. Student's own intelligence staff estimated a British garrison of no more than 5,000 and did not include the Commonwealth or Greek troops evacuated from Greece. The Germans assumed they had been withdrawn directly to Alexandria. Additionally, they estimated that no troops were positioned at Retimo, and only 400 at Heráklion, and that the Cretan population would enthusiastically welcome the Germans forces.[34]

Although some of this poor estimate of enemy strength can be attributed to overconfidence by the Germans which was understandable given their success to date, skillful camouflage and strict fire control preventing engagement of enemy reconnaissance aircraft by Freyberg's forces also contributed to the lack of intelligence. While it was a logical assumption of the German operational planners to expect that some British forces would be stationed at each of the three airfields, the capital of Canea and Suda Port, the true strength and disposition of forces was never fully appreciated until the battle commenced. The apparent absence of British positions and forces encountered by German reconnaissance was contradicted by Churchill's public statements that Crete would be defended at all costs by the British, therefore casting even greater doubt into Student's mind.

Student and Löhr, initially, were at odds over how the operation should be conducted. Löhr proposed securing the single objective of Máleme (see appendix B), then advancing from west to east to seize Suda Bay, Canea, Retimo and Heráklion along the coastal road. This would allow rapid reinforcement of the airfield and could be supported with overwhelming dive-bomber and fighter support from VIII *Fliegerkorps*. Student balked at this option as it allowed the enemy to concentrate at the point of contact, denigrated the advantages of vertical envelopment, and would result in a conventional ground battle of attrition that Student did not possess the time or resources to wage.[35]

Student proposed launching a parachute and glider operation to seize all three key airfields, Suda Bay, and Canea simultaneously, paralyzing the enemy and denying him the opportunity to deploy his reserve to counter all threats. Once an airfield had been secured, rapid reinforcement by airlanded troops and equipment would be undertaken. This plan, which had worked well in Holland, was known as the "oil spots" method with multiple objectives being seized simultaneously without a designated main effort, and then exploited to linkup with other forces. Student's plan had flaws in itself. He did not possess sufficient Ju52s with which to strike simultaneously at all targets, nor did Richthofen feel confident that he could provide air cover to support the dispersed location and number of objectives.[36]

With Student, Löhr and Richthofen all in disagreement, it fell to Göring to resolve the dispute. Based upon advice from his own staff, he directed a compromise of the two plans. Four objectives were to be taken in two waves, the western objectives of Máleme and Canea secured first followed by Heráklion and Retimo in the east. The plans had neither the concentration of force nor the shock effect and surprise that Student and Löhr had advocated, and was premised upon being able to rapidly turn around transport aircraft in-between sorties. Hitler intervened at this stage, fearing the British would destroy Crete's airfields in order to prevent air-landings, and directed that a seaborne force be included as insurance. Both Student and Löhr had been against including a seaborne component in the operation, and this late addition from Hitler in the compressed planning timeframe, placed additional pressure on planners to find, fit and incorporate naval forces into the plan.[37]

These factors taken into account, Student and Löhr produced a four-phased operation. Phase One would consist of preparatory bombardment by *VIII Fliegerkorps* in the week preceding D Day of all defensive locations on Crete, combined with air attacks on the RAF on Crete and the Royal Navy in the Aegean and Mediterranean Seas. This planned to ensure the Navy was neutralized prior to the sea reinforcement of Crete later in the operation and attain air superiority. Phase Two would be the critical parachute and glider assault by 7th *Flieger* Div to seize at least one airfield and neutralize antiaircraft guns. Approximately 100 dive bombers and fighter aircraft would then fly in to Máleme and Heráklion to support further operations. Phase Three would be the airlanding of the 5th *Gebirg* Div and the subsequent "mopping up" of resistance. Phase Four would be the seaborne reinforcement by elements of the 5th *Gebirg* Div and heavy equipment. In all, 15,750 airborne and 7,000 seaborne troops were to be involved supported by in excess of 600 combat aircraft.

Student's plan is best analyzed if considered by phase. On 14 May 1941, VIII *Fliegerkorps* commenced air attacks on Crete, targeting aircraft, antiaircraft guns, communications, and field defenses surrounding the airfields, Suda Bay and Canea. Long-range missions were also flown further south to mine the Suez Canal and Alexandria areas to hinder the Royal Navy providing support to the operation. Royal Navy shipping sheltering in Suda Bay was continually bombed and strafed, and HMS *York*, the British heavy cruiser, and 12 other ships lay damaged or sunk within five days. In a battle that pitted German airpower against British naval power, Richthofen gained the early advantage. By the start of the airborne invasion on 20 May 1941, the Royal Navy was able to conduct night operations only in the Aegean Sea and Suda Bay areas, and had to withdraw south outside of air range of bombers and fighters based in Greece by day, or face concentrated air attack. Runways and harbors were not targeted in order to preserve them for future airlanding and seaborne operations; however any movement by day on the island of personnel or vehicles drew immediate attack. Richthofen enjoyed a thirty to one numerical advantage in aircraft over the RAF stationed at Crete or that flew long-range sorties from North Africa. At the height of the preparatory battle on 16 May 1941 Richthofen was able to fly 500 bomber and fighter sorties against the defenses of Crete, and by 20 May 1941 could confidently claim that air superiority had been gained over Crete and the island had, by day, effectively been isolated from external naval support.[38]

Student divided Crete into three areas for the critical phase of the operation, the airborne assault (see appendix C for the order of battle and appendix D for schematic). *Gruppe West* (*Generalmajor* Eugen Meindl) consisted of the *Luftlande Sturmregiment* (less two companies), a company of antiaircraft machine-guns and over half the available gliders totaling 1,860 men. Meindl was tasked to seize Máleme airfield then retain it for follow-on airborne landings. He would be reinforced later the first day by one of the seaborne convoys carrying a 5th *Gebirg* Div battalion and heavy weapons, at which time he was to exploit to the east and link up with *Gruppe Mitte* around Canea. *Gruppe Mitte* (*Generalmajor* Wilhelm Süssmann) would parachute and land by glider in two waves. In the first wave 2,460 men from the 3rd *Fallschirmjäger* Regt, additional engineers, antiaircraft units and the remainder of the *Luftlande Sturmregiment* would land in vicinity of the Ayia Valley, and attack towards Canea and Suda Bay.

Student assessed (correctly) that Canea would be the likely location of the British headquarters and force reserve, and he tasked Süssmann with the destruction of both. Eight hours later, a second wave (made up of returning aircraft) consisting of 1,380 2nd *Fallschirmjäger* Regt troops would seize Retimo. At the same time *Gruppe Ost* (*Oberst* Bruno Bräuer) would parachute 2,360 men from the 1st *Fallschirmjäger* Regt reinforced with a remaining battalion from 2nd *Fallschirmjäger* Regt into Heráklion and seize the airfield and town. Like Meindl, Bräuer was to be later reinforced by a battalion-sized seaborne convoy. All objectives and landing zones were to be preceded by heavy bombers, dive-bombers and fighter-attack aircraft to neutralize enemy defenses.[39]

Critical to the success of this phase would be seizing and clearing the airfields, and neutralizing antiaircraft guns, therefore allowing dive bomber, fighter and transport aircraft to be flown in to continuing supporting the air and sea landings.

Ringel's 5th *Gebirg* Div was to have a limited role in the initial operation, with Student not foreseeing much of a role for the division on Crete other than mopping up resistance. Aside from detaching two battalions to the seaborne convoys reinforcing Máleme and Heráklion, Ringel's troops would remain in Greece until an airfield had been secured. They would then be committed as a division to that one area, and then exploit throughout the island from this lodgment. Ringel was not considered by Student to command any of the three assault sectors, nor did he see the need to deploy Ringel to Crete in any capacity as an overall land component commander. Student planned on commanding the initial phase of the campaign from Athens and then deploying to Crete on D+1 to assume overall command of the land operation on Crete from the individual sector commanders.[40]

The seaborne component of Student's plan was a poorly conceived aspect of the operation, and an afterthought imposed upon Student by Hitler. Student originally anticipated only utilizing transport ships to deliver stores, equipment, tanks and personnel not essential to the combat phase of the operation after the battle had been fought, and mine clearance of the port had been conducted. *Kriegsmarine* Commander of Naval Command South-East, *Generaladmiral* Karl-Georg Schüster possessed no German warships within the eastern Mediterranean to conduct the deployment or provide armed convoy protection. Schüster was able to secure the Italian destroyers *Lupo* and *Sagittario* for the operation as well as twelve torpedo boast and minesweepers. Approximately sixty-three Greek caiques (small motor-sailors) and seven freighters were requisitioned from the local area as transporters.

Ringel, given responsibility of organizing the move of two of his *Gebirg* battalions, light tanks and antiaircraft guns with which to protect the airfields once seized, formed two convoys each protected by an Italian destroyer. One convoy, the 1st Motor Sailing Flotilla, consisting 2,331 troops from both 5th *Gebirg* Div and remaining paratroopers from 7th *Flieger* Div[41] and equipment, planned to arrive on D Day and link up with the *Sturmregiment*. On D+1 the 2nd Motor Sailing Flotilla of similar size was to link up with *Gruppe Ost* at Heráklion. The remaining 5th *Gebirg* Div troops, equipment and Corps troops including an armored battalion, motorcycle battalion, and additional antiaircraft units would deploy by steamer once Suda Bay was secured.[42] Ringel was skeptical of the plan from the outset; his troops were alpine trained not marines, and the convoy escort provided little protection if the Royal Navy was encountered.[43] Deploying the convoy under the cover of darkness in an effort to evade the Royal Navy denied Ringel's convoys the protection German air superiority by day assured them. Student, never enamored to the sea component of the plan from the start, placed his faith in his airborne troop's ability to secure victory. The convoys arriving at Crete would merely reinforce success.

Student's plan had two critical aspects to be successful. Firstly, an airfield needed to be seized by the morning of the second day and antiaircraft defenses neutralized in order to begin reinforcing by airlanding the 5th *Gebirg* Div. Secondly, the enemy could not be allowed to deploy his mobile reserves against any of the airfields to counterattack. Student planned on deploying Ringel's division into whichever airfield could be secured, although by the allocation of his resources, it is apparent he favored either Máleme or Heráklion. An obvious criticism of Student's plan, when examining the concept, is the lack of designated parachute or glider-borne reserve for the operation. Student assumed, somewhat arrogantly, based upon the enemy estimates of his intelligence staff and the overwhelming air superiority he possessed, that he could secure at least one of the airfields with the troops he had allocated and then rapidly introduce the 5th *Gebirg* Div.

Student's plan did not allocate a main effort nor did he specifically attack the enemy's center of gravity which he correctly assessed as the mobile reserve force located at Canea. Rather his plan was constricted by the two-wave concept that his available transport assets allowed him, separated by an eight-hour pause while the transport aircraft returned to Greece to refuel and embark the second wave. By striking at objectives in the west first and then in the east eight hours later, he lost any chance of surprise when he attacked Retimo and Heráklion. Student's decision to conduct his parachute drops and glider landings directly onto the airfield objectives which he knew were defended, albeit in unknown strength, ensured that while he could achieve some shock action and quickly assault the enemy positions, he placed his assaulting forces within range of the defending British troops.

On the eve of the airborne invasion, 19 May 1941, Student was confident in the ability of XI *Fliegerkorps* to complete the mission. He and his staff had demonstrated impressive energy and drive in assembling a force consisting two combat divisions supported by over 1,000 transport and combat aircraft in little more than three weeks, despite the limitations imposed on them by Hitler and the priority assigned to Operation Barbarossa.

VIII *Fliegerkorps* had effectively isolated Crete by sea causing significant damage to not only Royal Navy vessels, but also sinking a number of ships carrying crucial ammunition, equipment and supplies that Freyberg needed for the defense of the island. The only fighters available under Freyberg's direct command had been destroyed by the *Luftwaffe* or had been driven from their bases in Crete. Total air superiority required for the parachute operation had not only been gained by the *Luftwaffe*, but had caused significant damage to Freyberg's communications, antiaircraft and field defenses. The bombing and strafing sorties of the *Luftwaffe* which had followed Freyberg from the evacuation in Greece three weeks earlier had intensified in the week preceding the invasion to increase the effect of shock and fatigue on the already battle-wearied defenders.[44]

In the 7th *Flieger* Div, Student possessed the elite troops of the *Luftwaffe;* highly trained, well-led, experienced, and combat-tested. All *Fallschirmjäger* regiments in the division had conducted successful airborne operations within the past year at battalion and above level. A strength of the training and leadership of the division, all troops and units knew regardless of where they landed, the task and mission of their unit, the requirement to retrieve parachuted weapons canisters and quickly link up with other units rapidly, and press the attack on the enemy. Initiative, improvisation and junior leadership on the ground were the cornerstone of the *Fallschirmjäger* soldier. Student's plan, whilst limited by the availability of transport aircraft to strike simultaneously at all his objectives, was bold, aggressive and planned to overcome the enemy's defenses with a combination of shock and surprise. Student's only problem, that he did not know at the time, was that Freyberg's forces were forewarned and waiting for them.

[1]*Generaloberst* Alfried Jodl (1890-1946) was the head of the Operations Section of the High Command of the Armed Forces (OKW), and deputy to the Chief of OKW, Field Marshal Wilhelm Keitel. Jodl is credited for being responsible for much of the planning of German campaigns during the war, however was not involved in the planning of Operation Barbarossa. Jodl signed the unconditional German nation surrender document at Rheims, France, and after the Nuremburg trials was hanged.

[2]Callum MacDonald, *The Lost Battle: Crete, 1941* (New York: The Free Press, 1993), 42.

[3]Department of the Army, Pamphlet, No. 20-260, *The German Campaigns in the Balkans (Spring 1941)* (Washington, DC: Center of Military History, November 1953), Appendix II.

[4]*Generalissimo* Fransico Franco (1892-1975) when the Spanish Chief of General Staff led a revolt against the ruling Popular Front in 1935, was named the Spanish head of state in 1936, and ruled as a dictator until 1975. Hitler met with Franco a number of times to try to get Spain to join the Axis, yet Franco's demands the rights to Gibraltar and French North Africa were too great a request. Franco adopted a pro-Axis non-belligerent stance initially during the war until returning to complete neutrality in 1943 when it was apparent Germany was no longer seen to be winning.

[5]Antony Beevor, *Crete: The Battle and the Resistance* (London, United Kingdom: John Murray Ltd., 1991), 72.

[6]Some historians argue that this was due to Mussolini's arrogance wanting to increase his influence with Hitler by proving Italian forces could conduct the operation without German support. Crete was seen as a geographical objective of the Italian Army that would be taken in sequence after the offensive was conducted on the mainland. In fairness this was a lucky deduction. Had an airborne offensive been undertaken against Crete in October 1940, it would have been met by the 15,000-strong Cretan V Division who, fully equipped and well-trained, had yet to deploy from the island to the mainland.

[7]Department of the Army, Pamphlet, No. 20-260, Appendix II.

[8]Ibid.

[9]*Generalfeldmarschal* Hermann Wilhelm Göring (1893-1946) was a World War I fighter ace, early member of the Nazi Party, founder of the Gestapo, and formal second-in command to Hitler throughout the war. Göring was named head of the Luftwaffe upon its creation in 1935, became the first Luftwaffe Field Marshal (*Generalfeldmarschal*) and was promoted to the rank *Reichmarschal* in 1941, the highest rank in the Reich which made him senior to all other commanders. After early successes of the *Luftwaffe* in

France and the Low Countries, Göring's military star would fade. The failure of the *Luftwaffe* to defeat the RAF in the Battle of Britain, in Operation Barbarossa and to stop the allied bombing campaign lost him influence with Hitler. Göring was a driving force behind the creation of German airborne forces, and often pushed for their inclusion in operations, or to be given opportunities to operate independently of the Army and other forces. Göring was a firm proponent of the 'Jewish Solution' and was the highest German commander to appear at the Nuremburg Trials. Göring committed suicide by cyanide poisoning two days before his planned execution.

[10]B. H. Liddell Hart, *The German Generals Talk* (New York: Quill, 1979), 154-163; and MacDonald, 58.

[11]See footnote in Chapter 1. for biography on Student.

[12]A. H. Farrar-Hockley, *Student* (New York: Ballantine Books Inc, 1973), 37-38.

[13]Christopher Ailsby, *Hitler's Sky Warriors: German Paratroopers in Action 1939-1945* (Virginia: Brassey's Inc., 2000), 13.

[14]Ibid., 18.

[15]Farrar-Hockley, 53; and Ailsby, 18.

[16]Farrar-Hockley, 56-62.

[17]Ibid., 63.

[18]Ibid., 69.

[19]Ibid., 73.

[20]John Keegan, *Intelligence in War* (New York: Vintage Books, 2002), 164.

[21]Conflicting stories exist about who shot Student. Some claim that it was an enemy sniper, while other reports state that it was a passing unit of the *SS Leibstandarte Adolf Hitler* who were unaware the city had fallen. Student was shot in the head, required six months of convalescence, only returning in January 1941. He was warned by doctors never to parachute again or deploy by glider.

[22]Department of the Army, Pamphlet, No. 20-232, *Airborne Operations: A German Appraisal* (Washington, DC: Centre of Military History, October 1951), 18-19.

[23]Farrar-Hockley, 81.

[24]Hanson W. Baldwin, *The Crucial Years 1939-1941* (New York: Harper and Row Publishers, 1976), 280-281.

[25] *Generaloberst* Alexander Löhr was an Austrian officer who commanded *Luftflotte* IV during the Polish and Balkans campaigns, including Operation Merkur. Löhr later became the Balkan theatre commander, then air commander in Italy, before being the commander of Army Group E in the Aegean and Greek area for the remainder of the war. Löhr was a respected air commander but had limited knowledge of ground operations. Löhr was found guilty of war crimes by a Yugoslav court and hanged in 1947.

[26] Liddell Hart, 159.

[27] MacDonald, 62-66.

[28] *General der Flieger Freiherr* (Baron) Wolfram von Richthofen (1895-1945) was a fighter ace in World War I and cousin to the famous Baron von Richthofen (Red Baron). An engineer in the interwar period he joined the *Luftwaffe* on creation and commanded *Luftwaffe* units up to Corps level in support of operations in Poland, the Low Countries and France. Richthofen's VIII Fliegerkorps fought against the RAF in the Battle of Britain in 1940 before being transferred to Poland in preparation for Operation Barbarossa. Ambitious and well-regarded in the *Luftwaffe*, Richthofen was promoted to become Germany's youngest *Generalfeldmarschal* in 1943. He developed a brain tumor later that year, and died in 1945. Source: Peter Antill, *Crete 1941: Germany's Lightening Airborne Assault* (Oxford, United Kingdom: 2005), 20-21.

[29] MacDonald, 69.

[30] Generalmajor Julius "Papa" Ringel served in the Austrian Army between 1909 and 1938, and assumed command of the 5th *Gebirg* Div upon its formation in October 1940. Ringel later commanded a Corps in 1944, and upon promotion to *General der Gebirgstruppen*, Korps Ringel which fought against the Soviet Union in Austria in 1945. Source: Peter Antill, *Crete 1941: Germany's Lightening Airborne Assault* (Oxford, United Kingdom: 2005), 21.

[31] Christopher Shores, Brian Cull, and Nicola Malizia, *Air War for Yugoslavia, Greece and Crete* (London, United Kingdom: Grub Street, 1987), 335.

[32] Baldwin, 281.

[33] Department of the Army, Pamphlet, No. 20-260, 5.

[34] Beevor, 80.

[35] MacDonald, 70.

[36] MacDonald, 70; and Ailsby, 56.

[37] MacDonald, 72.

[38] Baldwin, 283-286; and MacDonald, 79.

[39] Antill, 32-33; Beevor, 348; and MacDonald, 80.

[40] MacDonald, 80.

[41] Baldwin, 290.

[42] Daniel M. Davin, *Official History of New Zealand in the Second World War, 1939-45, Crete* (Wellington, New Zealand: War History Branch, Department of Internal Affairs, 1953), 84.

[43] Ibid., 72-73.

[44] Geoffrey Cox, A *Tale of Two Battles: A Personal Memoir of Crete and the Western Desert, 1941* (London, United Kingdom: William Kimber, 1987), 53.

CHAPTER 4

FREYBERG'S OPERATIONAL PLAN

> Any foothold, or success against the troops in any particular position must be immediately counterattacked.
>
> Major-General B. C. Freyberg VC

The thirtieth of April 1941 proved to be an important day when considering Freyberg's planning for the defense of Crete. Freyberg, recently arrived from Greece and in the midst of preparing for the evacuation of the remnants of 2nd NZ Div to Egypt, was summoned to a meeting with Wavell who had arrived from Cairo. Named the commander of CREFORCE at this meeting, Freyberg was given his orders for the defense of Crete, which he recalled as follows:

> 1. Crete was to be held.
> 2. General Wavell considered that the island would be attacked in the next few days.
> 3. The objectives of the air attack were considered to be the airfields at Heráklion and Máleme.
> 4. No additional air support would be forthcoming.
> 5. General Freyberg to command. Brigadier-General (previously Colonel) Stewart as Brigadier-General General Staff (BGS), Brigadier-General Brunskill as Deputy Adjutant and Quartermaster General (DA and QMG). General Weston to command British troops in Suda Bay area.
> 6. General Weston, Royal Marines pointed out that a seaborne landing was very probable, and that as far as he could see, the Royal Navy would not be able to do much about it. The Commander-in-Chief said he would talk it over with Admiral Cunningham.
> 7. Air Commodore D'Albiac said the RAF had nothing to offer us.
> 8. The object of the defense was defined as: "To deny to the enemy the use of Crete as an air base."[1]

Freyberg's initial skepticism at the ability to defeat a combined air and sea attack with no air cover given the resources on the island was compounded by Wavell's reply that he could not evacuate the island due to a lack of available shipping. Freyberg, at this time, was then briefed by Wavell on the Ultra intelligence that he was to be given as the CREFORCE Commander. This intelligence was gained (and named Ultra) from the British breaking the codes of the German Enigma machine, and therefore the ability to decrypt and decode German wireless signal transmissions. Wavell then ordered Freyberg not to mention Ultra to anybody, and not to act on information provided by the Ultra source alone for fear of alerting the Germans to the fact that the British had broken their codes.[2] Until the declassification of Ultra in 1974 Freyberg's staff thought, as did many other operational and tactical commanders during World War II, that the source of the intelligence was provided by human intelligence and not by decipherment of German codes.[3]

Ultra in May 1941 was in its infancy within the intelligence community, but was to have an enormous effect on the conduct of Allied operations in World War II. Codes, keys, ciphers and cryptography were not new inventions. However from World War I, when wireless transmissions began to be used (and intercepted), military forces have sought to better safeguard information by use of complex encipherment and cryptography. The German inventor Arthur Scherbius invented the most complete cipher machine to date in 1918 that could encipher and decipher automatically and mechanically and would come be known as the Enigma machine. It was portable and compact, therefore suitable to military operations and, with multiple encryptions numbering 10,000 billion possibilities, was thought to be unbreakable by its inventor and the German military.[4]

Enigma was broken however, first by the Poles using mathematical and mechanical solutions in the 1920s, and then increasingly by the British based upon shared information from Polish intelligence and their own efforts. Many of the developments and refinements made by the British in breaking Enigma were based on the competence (or lack thereof) of the German operators and security measures employed by each of the armed forces. The *Gestapo* key was never broken during the war and the Army and *Kriegsmarine* only on rare occasions. The *Luftwaffe* key, however, was broken on 6 January 1940 and would continue to be broken throughout the war therefore providing valuable intelligence on air operations even *prior* to the Battle of Britain commencing.[5] Later, in 1943, the British captured a German U boat and its Enigma machine complete with ciphers, providing even greater understanding to the German use of codes for maritime use.

Ultra was distributed from Bletchley Park, the home of the Codes and Cyphers School where intercepted German Enigma and other signal transmissions were decrypted, to a very limited distribution list. Initially this was restricted to Churchill and his military CinCs for each of the operational areas and services. Commanders were not briefed where the intelligence originated from, only to trust the source, until the Greek campaign when the CinCs were told of the source. Freyberg was to become, on Churchill's approval, the first commander below CinC level to receive Ultra intelligence.[6]

At the operational level, the restrictions placed upon acting solely on Ultra intelligence were evident in the battle that Admiral Cunningham undertook against the Italian Navy in March 1941 prior to the Battle of Matapan. Forewarned by Ultra gained through intercepts of the *Luftwaffe* Enigma signal traffic, Cunningham knew of the Italian fleet intentions to interdict a British convoy, their location at the time and their strength, including the air support plan to be provided by the *Luftwaffe*. However, unable to act based solely on the information gained by Ultra; Cunningham dispatched a flying boat on a reconnaissance mission to confirm the location of the Italian fleet. Only once the fleet's location was confirmed by a second source, did Cunningham proceed to engage and defeat the Italian fleet at Matapan destroying three cruisers and two destroyers.[7]

From Wavell's briefing on 30 April 1940 to the actual commencement of the parachute invasion, Freyberg would receive sixteen Ultra messages (see appendix E) relating to the planned *Luftwaffe* operation to seize Crete, arguably the best and most complete intelligence picture any commander at that stage of the war had of the enemy's intentions. Historians have disagreed since the conclusion of the battle about Freyberg's use of the intelligence provided to him, especially since the declassification of Ultra in 1974. Prior to this many historians (including Davin) concluded, based upon the official unit histories and personal accounts of the commanders, that the British defense of Crete was an admirable defeat in which the officers and soldiers did the best they could in trying conditions. The declassification of Ultra allowed historians (Beevor and Lewin are examples) to re-examine the battle from a different perspective that Freyberg had such forewarning of the invasion that he should have been victorious, regardless of the other influences on the battle (including enemy air superiority, the state of the troops, and the lack of equipment). In recent years, historians (Freyberg's son understandably, Keegan, Lewin, and Bennett amongst them) have continued to examine the influence of both the intelligence provided to Freyberg and his ability to make decisions based upon it given the security restrictions placed upon him, and the operational considerations of the entire battle.

The four most contentious issues regarding Freyberg's use of Ultra are: that he misread the intelligence signals provided; that regardless of the intelligence he was unable to fully employ it due to the security restrictions imposed upon him; that whilst Ultra provided him information it did not provide him intelligence; and lastly, that regardless of the intelligence provided, he did not possess sufficient force to win the battle.

Beevor contends that Freyberg misread Ultra signals and therefore arrayed his forces primarily against a seaborne invasion, at the expense of defending in strength against an airborne attack at Máleme. OL 2168, which gives the impression of three mountain regiments deploying by sea instead of the original one, supposedly strengthened Freyberg's assumption that a seaborne force would be a decisive factor in the battle.[8] The seaborne assault was confirmed by the preparation of twelve ships carrying 27,000 tons of equipment and personnel moving from Naples, to which Freyberg was alerted on 11 May 1941. Freyberg was informed through Ultra on 18 May 1941 that the convoy had departed the Piraeus for Crete. The convoy is not reported on again until the battle has commenced, therefore Freyberg was right to consider it the likelihood of a seaborne attack within his defensive plan.[9]

That Freyberg considered a seaborne invasion in conjunction with an airborne one to be imminent was not unreasonable. The initial appreciation of the defense conducted by Weston, the briefing received from Wavell on 30 April 1941, that Suda Bay had specifically not been mined by the Germans, and the Ultra signals in the three weeks leading to the invasion, all pointed to a seaborne component of the attack. Freyberg could hardly ignore a force of up to 10,000 troops complete with tanks, antiaircraft guns and artillery arriving at Crete some time, and at undetermined locations, after the first landings by parachute and glider on D Day. That an island had never been taken from the air alone before in the history of warfare must also have played upon Freyberg's mind as a military commander when considering the deployment of his defenses. Whilst not short of personnel to oppose an airborne and seaborne attack, lacking transportation, heavy weapons and tanks Freyberg did not possess the resources to rapidly switch from one threat to the other.

Lewin adds weight to Beevor's argument appropriating blame on Freyberg, theorizing that he did not possess the mental capacity to process the information that Ultra provided him, in essence "he got the message, but not the meaning". Churchill wrote at the time "at no moment during the war was our intelligence so precisely informed". Freyberg, however, failed to appreciate the (correct) method in which Student would reinforce the initial parachute invasion and misunderstood that Máleme was to be the main effort for the attack. Further, Freyberg did not deduce that the initial force of 10,000 airborne troops was Student's only method of seizing the critical initial point of entry thus allowing reinforcement, and if defeated would secure the British victory.[10] This judgment, however, can only be made in hindsight, as Student had not determined that this would be the point of his reinforcement until the second day of the battle. Lewin neatly examines the context of the battle only in relation to the effect of Ultra on it and pays only scant attention to the other operational and environmental influences at the time. He does, however, concede that the value of Ultra intelligence greatly diminishes in value if the enemy possesses other significant superiority.[11] Given the effect of overwhelming air superiority that has already been discussed in an earlier chapter, it is not unreasonable to balance his argument with the influence that Richthofen's VIII *Fliegerkorps* had on the battle.

As with Cunningham's knowledge of the Italian fleet's intentions prior to the Battle of Matapan, Freyberg was somewhat hamstrung by what he could achieve with the Ultra intelligence. Ultra signals would be sent to Crete from Bletchley Park to Group Captain Beamish, the Air Officer Commanding Crete, decoded, and then handed to Freyberg. Freyberg, upon reading the contents, had to then destroy them immediately. Additionally, Freyberg was not to discuss the contents with any of his staff or subordinates. With no secondary means to confirm the intelligence provided, he was rendered incapable by the security restrictions of acting on the intelligence as one could have expected if this restriction was not placed upon him.[12]

This is most evident in Freyberg's disposition of forces to defend against a seaborne and airborne attack. The early intelligence provided during the period when Freyberg assumed command on 30 1941 and the receipt of OL 2170 (see appendix E) on 7 May 1941 all point to a combined attack. Therefore, Freyberg, when he issued CREFORCE Order No. 10 (see appendix F) on 3 May 1941, outlined his disposition of forces to meet both these threats. OL 2170 and subsequent signals give stronger indications that the attack will be predominantly by air, and while Freyberg made some changes in unit disposition, he did not drastically alter his defensive positions. Two reasons support this Freyberg's action. Firstly, Freyberg did not possess the troops to physically cover all possible airborne landing and drop zones, and therefore had to rely on an economy of force operation utilizing quick and mobile reserves. Had he dispersed troops to cover more potential drop zones, Freyberg would have been "chasing ground" and fragmenting his defense. Secondly, under the Ultra restrictions placed upon him, some historians (including his son Paul, who complied Freyberg's biography based upon interviews with him prior to his death and Freyberg's personal notes) conclude that Freyberg was unable to effect large shifts in subordinate unit disposition without the chance of alerting enemy reconnaissance and possibly agents on the island that he had forewarning of the invasion plan.

Hindsight, again, is cruel to Freyberg in this regard. An area to the west of the Tavronitis River close to Máleme airfield was not occupied during the initial deployment of 5th NZ Bde. Freyberg, and his subordinate commanders were aware of the deficiency in the plan, and according to Paul Freyberg, Freyberg intended to deploy a Greek battalion into the gap. Additionally, he planned to change the dispositions of both the 4th NZ Bde and 5th NZ Bde to cover the area with greater depth and mutual support, changing the orientation of the defense from the seaborne threat to concentrating against the airborne attack. However, with the security restrictions faced by Freyberg, he was unwilling to do so without consent from Wavell. Paul Freyberg writes that Freyberg sent secure messages to Wavell seeking the reduction of the Ultra security restrictions that would enable him to change the dispositions prior to the battle. Wavell's reply on 13 May 1941 stated that the rule could not be relaxed because "the authorities in England would prefer to lose Crete rather than risk jeopardizing Ultra."[13] As all secret documentary evidence was destroyed upon reading during the battle, it is impossible to support or refute what Paul Freyberg contends happened between Wavell and Freyberg. Regardless, no further action was taken to move troops into the Tavronitis River area.[14] This would become, in the airborne invasion, the one landing area at Máleme for both glider and parachutists to be free from enemy fire and observation, therefore allowing them to concentrate and conduct their attack to seize the airfield.

Incredulous as it may seem that Freyberg placed the security of British intelligence sources above that of his troops on the ground as it appears in hindsight, this opinion must be balanced with two considerations. Firstly, there was Freyberg himself, a career military professional who accepted the responsibility of commanding CREFORCE with its shortfalls in equipment and support, but nevertheless was also fiercely loyal to the military chain of command and its processes. Freyberg understood the strategic conduct of warfare and having seen the might of the German army in Greece and North Africa, knew that the war could not conclude rapidly in favor of the Allies. Therefore with British successes over the Germans minimal at that stage of the war, the importance of Ultra could not be overstated. Secondly, Freyberg's defensive plan was oriented to take into account the geographical shortfalls of his dispositions, namely counterattack forces allocated within each of his subordinate units.

More recently, historians such as Bennett and Keegan have tended to look at Ultra as nearly giving the British victory on Crete despite the limitations of the operational environment they faced.[15] Keegan points to both OL 2170 and OL 2/302 as examples of *information* provided as opposed to *intelligence* by Bletchley Park. The OL signals fail to indicate which units, and their strength, would land at what locations, therefore not designating the main effort of the expected attack into what location. Many historians also gloss over the fact that Heráklion was a better developed runway on Crete, capable of sustaining all *Luftwaffe* aircraft types, whereas Máleme was a temporary runway still under improvement by the British. Máleme did possess the advantage of its proximity to

Suda Bay, and therefore seaborne reinforcement by heavier freighters and resupply vessels once secured, and the capital. Hindsight again plays its part when analyzing these two objectives. Freyberg was expected to defend *all* landing zones. The fact that Máleme would be the point where the main effort would be was not known to either Freyberg *or* Student prior to the battle.

The ability of Bletchley Park to intercept, decrypt, translate and then interpret information in the early stages of the war was limited. Raw information was not able to be passed from Bletchley Park to operational commanders for their own analysis owing to the security restrictions of Ultra. Bennett concludes that Bletchley Park could make quick translations of Enigma intercepts; however they did not possess the experience to collate all the available information into precise military intelligence able to be used by field commanders.[16] Keegan goes further to conclude that "the crucial synthesis of the German operation order, OL 2/302 of 13 May 1941, the work of the Bletchley interpreters, not the transcripts of the German intercepts themselves, leaves it unspecified how the Assault Regiment and the nine battalions of Parachute Regiments 1, 2 and 3 are to be allocated between targets."[17]

Regardless of the quantity or quality of information that was provided to Freyberg prior to the battle, it is clearly evident that he possessed a significant intelligence advantage over the Germans. Ultra provided him with a more detailed picture of the enemy intent and plan than any other battle to date in the war. Crete also proved however, that intelligence can not overcome all other factors in battle; be they planning, leadership, manning and equipment, training, morale, or merely a superior enemy force. Ultra did much to confirm the original deployment of the defense prior to OL 2170, based upon initially Weston and then Freyberg's appreciation of ground, the key terrain, and the enemy threat. The addition of Ultra intelligence through the first weeks of May altered Freyberg's planning and disposition of forces, although with the security restrictions placed on him, and the troops he had available, Freyberg was in no way assured of the victory that some historians argue Ultra should had given him.

As Freyberg's intelligence picture provided by Ultra developed in the three weeks prior to the invasion, so did his appreciation of the ground, the capabilities of his subordinate units, and the difficulties he would face constituting an integrated and supportable defense. An examination of Freyberg's operational planning needs to take into account four factors (additional to intelligence) in the lead-up to the German D Day; his appreciation and method of defense, the orders that he issued, his changes in the plan as information became available, and the actions of his subordinate commanders to implement his orders.

Firstly, it must be remembered that Freyberg arrived in Crete as the division commander of 2nd NZ Div, not a corps commander of a multinational and multi-service force that he was to command on the island.[18] Often in historical analysis after Crete have writers concentrated on Freyberg's planning, orders and leadership in relation only to the New Zealand division, and not as the overall ground force commander. This is an important factor, when considering Freyberg's relationship both with his subordinate commanders of all units and in the planning and conduct of the battle, especially when looking to subsequently apportion blame or culpability for actions that occurred on the battlefield.

The Battle of Crete was Freyberg's first command above division level in World War II, but it was not his last. As a corps commander, Freyberg received mixed appraisals throughout World War II from his superiors and subordinates alike. Detractors, including General Sir Claude Auchinleck and General Mark Clark,[19] saw Freyberg as too cautious, meddlesome, a prima donna, and a micromanager. However, Freyberg also had many supporters. Churchill and Wavell rated Freyberg as an able commander, as did subordinates including Brigadier-General Howard Kippenberger.[20] Rommel found Freyberg to possess drive and aggression, and throughout subsequent operations in North Africa and Italy, Freyberg demonstrated the ability to think laterally and develop plans to coordinate air and ground operations at Corps level, adapting and overcoming the *Blitzkrieg* tactics of the enemy.[21]

For a commander to conduct detailed and adequate planning, he requires a staff capable of assisting him in the development and implementation of plans. Freyberg possessed such a staff in HQ 2nd NZ Div, which had been formed and staffed from early 1940 when Freyberg had assumed command of 2NZEF. This staff planned and conducted the division's concentration and training in the North Africa desert in 1940, and the operations in Greece in April 1941. They were aware of the nuances of Freyberg's command and leadership style, and the capabilities of the subordinate brigades. For the Battle of Crete, Freyberg was without this valuable command tool. Freyberg had lost his divisional staff (and his best and most complete infantry brigade, the 6th NZ Bde) complete with much needed communications equipment at Suda Bay on 29 April 1941. The evacuation of these two elements by Middle East Command to Alexandria that same day, and one day before Freyberg was named as the CREFORCE Commander did not sit well with Freyberg at the time or after the war. He would later write:

> The naval convoy, with our well organized units, lay all day on 29 April in Suda Bay, and at dusk left, taking my Divisional Headquarters and the fine Infantry Brigade. By the time I took over command of Crete on 30 April, this valuable part of the New Zealand Division had already arrived in Alexandria. For all these mistakes – for which Whitehall, the Commanders-in-Chief Middle East and W Force and their staffs were responsible – we were to pay a high price.[22]

Without his own staff, Freyberg looked to the existing CREFORCE Headquarters but found little assistance from General Weston, the incumbent commander. Weston, who was relegated to commanding the MNBDO and the Suda Bay sector at the 30 April 1941 meeting with Wavell, Wilson and Freyberg, took his existing staff with him to this command. Freyberg was left with a corps-level headquarters consisting "no Staff, Signals or Clerks" and almost no command infrastructure or communications. Freyberg, through Brigadier-General Keith Stewart as a Chief of Staff, constituted a headquarters from what officers and soldiers he could of the units that had arrived on Crete, and what troops could be released from Acting/Major-General Edward Puttick's[23] 2nd NZ Div HQ. While Freyberg considered them to be fine troops who worked well, they were by no means an adequate Force HQ staff capable of planning and commanding a corps-sized operation.[24] Freyberg established his headquarters in the existing CREFORCE HQ location in a quarry two kilometers north-east of Canea. Although physically isolated from the bulk of the fighting troops occupying the Suda Bay and Canea areas, the position in an old quarry afforded Freyberg a grandstand view of the entire northern coastline from Canea to Máleme. Although seen by some of Freyberg's staff as being an obvious target, the quarry was not attacked by the *Luftwaffe* during the battle.[25] The headquarters was connected to subordinate units by landline and to Middle East Command by a wireless radio unit co-located with the headquarters.

Freyberg's initial appreciation for Crete was premised upon the direction he had received from Wavell, his own ground reconnaissance conducted immediately after the orders group on 30 April 1941, and three documents he received on 1 May 1941. These consisted of the appreciation conducted by Generals Watson and Wilson (who spent four days on Crete after evacuating from Greece), the initial estimation of the German Order of Battle believed to be in Southern Greece, and the British War Cabinet Joint Intelligence Committee (JIC) Appreciation.[26] The scale of the airborne and seaborne attack envisaged by all three appreciations quickly led Freyberg to conclude that he could not hold the island with the resources under his command, notably the lack of air support and the inability of the Royal Navy to guarantee repulsion of a seaborne invasion. After his initial reconnaissance, Freyberg remained doubtful of the ability of CREFORCE to defeat the German attack:

> The men had to be told the urgency of the situation in a way that would prepare them for the battle which was now about to burst upon them. At the same time, it was important to say nothing that would reveal my grave doubts as to our ability to hold Crete. Only five people at the time on Crete knew the seriousness of our position. In addition to myself they were General Weston, my Chief of Staff (Brigadier-General Stewart), my Personal Assistant (Captain John White) who typed my cables, and the Cypher Officer, who coded and decoded all high-grade cipher messages. These men were secure, and kept their doubts to themselves. I hope that my attitude was soldierly, and that outwardly I managed to look the part of a man with complete confidence in the situation.[27]

Freyberg dispatched two immediate signals to this effect, one to Wavell as the CREFORCE commander seeking additional resources and a second signal as Commander 2NZEF to Prime Minister Fraser to inform him of the situation. Freyberg recommended to both, that unless additional support was made available, serious consideration to evacuating Crete should be considered.[28] While Freyberg continued to use whatever political and command leverage he could with his superiors to improve the resources available for the battle, he undertook his own appreciation for the defense.

The geography of Crete has been discussed in a previous chapter, so it is sufficient to conclude that Freyberg, as the other commanders had deduced before him, saw no possibility of physically defending the entire island from seaborne and airborne attack. The distance between what Freyberg deduced to be the five pieces of key terrain on Crete coupled with the poor state of the only trafficable road meant a sector defense would have to be adopted. Freyberg identified the key terrain that must be defended as being the three airfields at Heráklion, Retimo and Máleme; the port at Suda Bay; and the capital of Canea. Of the three airfields, Heráklion being the most geographically isolated would need to be resourced, replenished and fought almost as an independent battle. The single road from Canea was sure to be targeted for interdiction by the enemy, therefore preventing the rapid reinforcement by reserves or a counterattack force to support Heráklion.[29]

Freyberg conceded that the Germans must hold the initiative at least at the start of the battle given they had choice of air and sea landing areas, however he and his subordinate commands would wrest that from them with immediate offensive action and initiative of their own demonstrated at the lowest levels of command. Every opportunity to prevent the enemy from concentrating and achieving cohesion was the cornerstone of Freyberg's defensive appreciation. A defense based upon static positions at each of the five key locations named above, coupled with mobile counterattack reserves to rapidly destroy forces on the ground formed the basis of Freyberg's plan. Static defenses would be well-camouflaged and engage gliders, transport aircraft, and parachutists while mobile reserves at all levels of command would counterattack, supported by tanks and artillery to destroy troops landed by air or lodgments by sea. Preventing the enemy from attaining a lodgment and therefore rapid reinforcement was critical.[30]

Freyberg also adopted the counterattack method to prevent such a lodgment that the previous CREFORCE headquarters had directed to subordinate brigades defending the airfields on 29 April 1941. CREFORCE Operation Order No. 2 directed:

> It is considered that the best method of defending an Airfield against an air-borne attack is to combine perimeter defense with a mobile column. A suitable disposition is two battalions or similar proportion for perimeter defense, and a third battalion mobile. The best location for the mobile battalion is such a distance outside the perimeter that they are comparatively immune from the preliminary air attacks on the Airfield and the perimeter. When these attacks are completed, the Commander of the Mobile column must use his best judgement to as to the best moment to move into attack.[31]

As Freyberg concluded his initial appreciation, he also had to consider the current disposition of forces on Crete. Freyberg was amongst the last convoys to reach the island, therefore the deployment of troops prior to 30 April 1941 had been made by Weston as the then CREFORCE commander. Weston, like Freyberg, was under the impression that troops evacuated from Greece in the last week of April 1941 would be soon withdrawn from Crete, and likely replaced by the 6th British Div, fresh from Egypt.[32] As the units arrived from Greece, Weston supplemented his own available MNBDO forces and two attached British infantry battalions protecting Suda Bay, and the Heráklion and Máleme airfields. The arrival of 4th NZ Bde, 5th NZ Bde and 19th Aust Bde in the four days preceding Freyberg saw Weston allocate each of these brigades defensive locations at Canea, Máleme and Retimo respectively.

Freyberg issued his first order, CREFORCE Order No. 3, upon assumption of command confirming the current dispositions in four sectors and the chain of command (see appendix G). This order effectively communicated the command status between CREFORCE and the Sector Commanders, however, at a lower level a lack of understanding of command relationships and failure to comply with this direction were evident. This existed where Weston had placed Bofors antiaircraft gun crews who reported directly to MNBDO and not to the Sector Commander. A similar situation existed for the RAF units at each of the airfields. They were "in location" and did not take direction from the ground commander for defensive measures. This was highlighted at Máleme where Bofors guns and RAF ground components were not tied into the overall defensive plan of Lieutenant-Colonel Leslie Andrew's 22nd Bn, despite Andrew's requests that they were. It is contestable if Freyberg, as an operational level commander, even knew of this discrepancy at the time; however, the attack onto Máleme airfield would expose this weakness in the defensive plan.[33]

On 3 May 1941, Freyberg issued CREFORCE Operation Order No. 10 (appendix F.) which directed the defense of Crete.[34] The order itself was simple and direct. The defense was to be conducted by sector with each allocated sufficient resources (from what was available) to conduct a static defense and retain a designated reserve with which to counterattack. A force reserve would be retained within the Canea area to conduct counterattacks into the Suda Bay, Máleme and Retimo sectors. Freyberg addresses both the seaborne and airborne threats within this order, with greater emphasis placed upon defending against an air assault than a seaborne attack.

Controlling an operational area as large as Crete presented to Freyberg, he was forced to conduct reorganization and redeployment of his forces almost as soon as CREFORCE Order No. 10 was issued. On 3 May 1941, Freyberg directed the acting 2nd NZ Div commander Acting/Major-General Puttick to change the disposition of the Hargest's 5th NZ Bde to provide stronger airfield defense and mutual support between battalions at Máleme Airfield and to better constitute a counterattack force. Later, under advice from Puttick, he approved the formation of a further brigade (10th NZ Composite Bde) to be formed from within the division to provide command and control of a number of "orphan" units in the Canea area, and to allow 4th NZ Bde to assume divisional and force reserve responsibilities.[35]

By 10 May 1941, Freyberg had completed the major redeployment of his forces (less those that would arrive from Egypt on 17 May 1941) and, as stated earlier in this chapter, was reluctant to conduct further deployments for security reasons surrounding Ultra. A summary of the strengths and weaknesses of the physical disposition of his major units (see appendix H) at 19 May 1941 leads to the following conclusions. Firstly in the Heráklion sector, 14th Infantry Bde under Brigadier-General Brian Chappel[36] consisting four infantry battalions and two Greek regiments, reinforced by six light tanks and two heavy tanks, were dug in around the airfield. Both Freyberg and Chappel were aware of the sector's isolation from reinforcement once battle commenced, and therefore additional artillery, infantry and armoured resources had been allocated to assist the isolated defense, and to retake the airfield by counterattack if required. Replenishment was conducted by ship into a small port at Heráklion by the Royal Navy nightly.[37]

At Retimo, Brigadier-General George Vasey[38] had deployed his forces to not only defend the Retimo airfield and town, but also to maintain a link along the Canea-Retimo-Heráklion coastal road, from which he could expect reinforcement by the force reserve counterattack troops if required. Additionally, two Australian battalions guarded the beach at Geogioupolis, the most likely landing site on the northern coast. Retimo was not seen as important an airfield as Máleme or Heráklion, however possession of the road linking the sectors was crucial to the integrity of Freyberg's defense.

Suda Sector, commanded by Major-General Weston, concentrated the majority of its combat power within the Suda Bay area protecting the port and denying a seaborne attack in the sector. Weston was also responsible for all antiaircraft guns and coastal artillery; therefore his ground troop disposition reflected protecting these valuable resources. Concentrated ground attack against the Suda Sector would require the committal of the reserve to retake the Port or to oppose a beach lodgment.[39]

4th NZ Bde commanded by Brigadier-General Lindsay Inglis,[40] was situated two kilometers west of Canea, and designated as the force reserve. Although only two battalions in strength, Inglis' force was to be reinforced by the Welch regiment on command of HQ CREFORCE. Inglis had an unenviable task. His brigade was to dig in and be prepared to fight from fixed positions, but be capable of being committed quickly in a counterattack toward Máleme to the west, into the Canea township itself or to the east to support 19th Aust Bde or in an extreme situation; the Heráklion airfield.[41] Freyberg allocated most of the limited mobility assets that existed on the island to the force reserve. CREFORCE Operation Instructions No. 13 (issued on 15 May 1941) and No. 16 (issued on 18 May 1941) dedicated sufficient transport assets to the force reserve to move two infantry battalions (the 18th and 19th Bns) and the brigade headquarters. Additionally, ten light tanks from the 3rd Hussars and a Light Troop of Royal Artillery constituted the counterattack force. The planning priorities given to Inglis as the reserve force commander were to the Máleme-Suda area, followed by Retimo and lastly Heráklion.[42]

10th NZ Bde commanded by Brigadier-General Kippenberger was formed on 14 May 1941 to provide command and control of a number of units that were without a formal headquarters or who had been reformed as infantry from the artillery and service support units without equipment. Consisting only one regular infantry battalion (the 20th Bn from 4th NZ Bde), a composite battalion, and two Greek regiments, the brigade occupied defensive positions between Inglis' 4th NZ Bde to their east and 5th NZ Bde in the vicinity of Plantanias. Kippenberger also provided depth to the defense of Canea by occupying the Ayia Valley, a high speed approach from the south-west directly into the township of Canea. Kippenberger's force, short of equipment and ammunition, had the additional task of providing a battalion-sized divisional reserve to 2nd NZ Div capable of attacking west to Máleme or to reinforce 4th NZ Bde to the east.[43]

Brigadier-General James Hargest[44] commanded 5th NZ Bde, the most complete fighting force on the island, consisting four infantry battalions and a Greek regiment plus supporting tanks, infantry and artillery. Hargest, after Freyberg and Puttick's initial redeployment of his troops, deployed 22nd Bn on and around Máleme airfield with 21st and 22nd Bns further east, defending against a seaborne assault and in a position to conduct a counterattack onto Máleme airfield or the surrounding areas. The 28th (Maori) Bn was held four kilometers east of Máleme protecting HQ 5th Bde and the small town of Plantanias.[45] The 1st Greek Regiment under command of 5th NZ Bde was deployed 12 kilometers further west of Máleme protecting the natural beach landing at Kisamos Kastelli bay from seaborne assault. Within Hargest's sector there were also a number of units without formal command structures, including remnants of the RAF ground detachment and Fleet Air Arm at Máleme.

Two flaws are immediately apparent in the deployment of Hargest's brigade. Firstly the failure to physically cover the Tavronitis River area which has previously been discussed; and secondly, the location of Hargest's headquarters five kilometers from Máleme airfield and the majority of his fighting units. Hargest placed himself in a position as a commander where, if what little communications that existed were cut between his subordinate units and headquarters, he would have no means of commanding his brigade nor reinforcing his forward units or coordinating a counterattack. Hargest may have been wary of being cut off from his higher headquarters, hence his headquarters location, however this placed him and the 28th (Maori) Bn at least a one-hour march from the airfield and the remainder of his brigade.[46]

Within Freyberg's subordinate units, preparation for the defense continued, confined by the limited resources that could be brought in by the Royal Navy and the increasing air attacks by the *Luftwaffe*. Rehearsals and planning for counterattacks depended on the commander of each unit. Puttick's division headquarters issued its own operation order on 5 May 1941, stressing the importance of the counterattack both within each brigade and at the division and force level. 4th NZ Bde directed in Operation Instruction No. 8 that "battalions detail companies to conduct counterattacks against enemy landings on the initiative of their commanders",[47] while a 5th NZ Bde orders group directed that "in the event of the enemy making an airborne or seaborne attack in any part of the area, to counterattack and destroy him immediately."[48]

A failing of Freyberg's subordinate units during the preparation for the battle was the lack of detailed rehearsals that were conducted between units, although reconnaissance and coordination occurred between staffs. Within the Máleme Sector, officers of individual units such as the 22nd and 21st Bns of the 5th NZ Bde conducted reconnaissance of routes to support each other and established signal flares to launch the counterattack in case of communication failure. Lieutenant Colonel Andrew VC,[49] commanding 22nd Bn, additionally undertook an aerial reconnaissance to determine enemy approaches to Máleme airfield.[50] Whilst this reconnaissance was conducted, detailed rehearsals by day and night did not occur within 5th NZ Bde. 4th NZ Bde, as the force reserve, conducted reconnaissance from its location to each of the sectors but did not commit to full rehearsals to either Máleme or Canea, nor Retimo or Heráklion sectors. While constant air attack by the *Luftwaffe* made this near impossible to conduct by day, a defense that had such limited communications and relied upon counterattacking across and through other unit lines should have had greater coordination.

Even though Freyberg's plan was simple, and in theory operationally sound, two aspects that were critical to its success would plague him in the preparation for the battle, and greatly influence its outcome. In order to counterattack effectively within each sector, and decide when and where to commit his own force reserve, Freyberg needed two capabilities; mobility and communications. What mobility assets Freyberg possessed, he allocated to each of the sectors, with the majority to the force reserve. His distribution of tanks to each sector (the majority of tanks only arrived between 16 and 19 May 1941) also reflected his desire for individual units to conduct quick counterattacks and not to wait for reinforcement from a higher headquarters. Given the poor maintenance state of the light and heavy tanks on the island, Freyberg can hardly be accused of dividing this valuable combat power. Most tanks were incapable of traveling ten kilometers without mechanical failure, so their retention as a strong central armored counterattack force was pointless.

Freyberg was unable to procure enough communication equipment, especially wireless sets, prior to the battle to equip all units. Although reasonable communications existed between CREFORCE headquarters and the sector commanders, poor communications from brigade to battalion and lower slowed the passage of information. There was little Freyberg could do to mitigate this fact. Freyberg has been criticized by some historians for placing his headquarters too far from Máleme and Canea in the lead up to the battle. However, Freyberg (rightly so) was conscious of maintaining his geographical position to influence the battle as the CREFORCE commander *not* the 2nd NZ Div commander. Establishing his headquarters within Puttick's divisional area would have hindered his ability to command the *whole* operation, including the Retimo and Heráklion sectors.

While Freyberg finalized preparations for the defense of Crete, he continued to face resistance over a further issue with Wavell, the RAF and Whitehall. Middle East Command was reluctant to allow Freyberg to deny the runways to the enemy at the three airfields by demolitions. By 19 May 1941, Freyberg had directed all aircraft depart Crete (only a maximum of 13 were operating in the week previously), and argued that destroying the runways would assist in defeating reinforcement by airlanding troops and equipment. The position taken by the RAF and Middle East Command was that the runways would be needed for further use later in the war. The authority to conduct the demolitions requested by Freyberg lay with the Chief of Air Staff at Whitehall, and was not given prior to the battle.[51] Even if it had, it is unlikely that CREFORCE would have been unable to deny the use of the runways to future German airlanding, possessing neither sufficient equipment, explosives nor time to render them inoperable. This was confirmed after the battle in the United Kingdom Chiefs of Staff response to Prime Minister Fraser about the issue, stating that an engineer company with mechanical augers would take twenty-four to thirty hours and seven and one-half tons of explosives per runway to complete, none of which were available on Crete.[52] Destroyed equipment and vehicles were placed on the runways as obstructions prior to the attack; however these were only effective until troops were able to clear them from the fields, which was one of the tasks assigned to airborne and airlanding units.

Once Freyberg had set his defensive positions, there was little he could do except refine the preparations for the battle and continue to extort Wavell for additional air support. Freyberg toured Crete constantly, reviewing preparations with subordinate commanders and talking with his troops. When asked by soldiers how to deal with the paratroopers, he replied "just fix bayonets and go at them as hard as you can."[53] On the eve of the German invasion, CREFORCE had completed what preparations could be made. The *Luftwaffe* had intensified its air attacks over the previous week on Crete described in Chapter Three, and driven the RAF from the island. Additionally, the daily bombing and strafing of ground forces known as the "hate"[54] had begun reducing what communications landlines that existed between units, limiting movement by day, and contributing to weaken the state of mind of the defenders. Captain Geoffrey Cox, one of Freyberg's intelligence officers, recalled his thoughts on the impending invasion after Hargest commented on the eve of the battle, "I don't know what lies ahead. I only know that it produces in me a sensation I never knew in the last war. It is not fear. It is something quite different, something which I can only describe as dread:"[55]

> I did not need to question him on these words. I knew exactly what he meant. His was the reaction of a thoughtful man – and a man of proven bravery – to the extraordinary phenomenon of this period of the war, to the mystique, indeed the mystery which seemed to surround Germany's staggering success in the field. We were in the path of a military machine which had smashed Poland in a matter of days, and overwhelmed France, Belgium, Holland and the BEF in a matter of weeks. The RAF and the Royal Navy had checked it at the Channel, but it had turned south-east and had swept through Yugoslavia and Greece like an avalanche. In the western desert only a few German tanks and a previously little known general called Erwin Rommel had been needed to rout the British Army which had, three months before, routed the Italians. Now, this evening, over this golden and blue horizon, these same apparently irresistible forces were massing in an even more novel form to descend on us.[56]

Freyberg's Operational Order No. 10, issued over two weeks prior was explicit in its instruction of how to defeat the German invasion, and the counterattack intent communicated, if not adequately rehearsed to the lowest levels. Ultra had provided Freyberg with a comprehensive understanding of the expected enemy attack, although on the eve of the battle, he could still not be sure of the location where the main effort for the attack would occur.

Freyberg had arrayed his forces to defend against the two threats that Ultra and his own experience dictated; a heavy airborne assault supported by a seaborne attack. Where possible, Freyberg had allocated resources and equipment to each sector commander in order for them to constitute a strong static defensive position, and more importantly a counterattack force capable of retaking key terrain and denying an enemy lodgment on the island. Despite the shortages in equipment, ammunition and most importantly air support, Freyberg was confident that "at least we will give an excellent account of ourselves, and with the help of the Royal Navy I trust that Crete will be held."[57]

---

[1]Paul Freyberg, *Bernard Freyberg VC: Soldier of Two Nations* (Kent, United Kingdom: Hodder and Stoughton, 1991), 267.

[2]Ibid., 268.

[3]Sir John White, interviewed by Sergeant Brenton Beach, 8 March 2004, interview 7a, transcript, Queen Elizabeth II Army Memorial Museum Veterans Oral History Project, Waiouru, New Zealand.

[4]John Keegan, *Intelligence in War* (New York: Vintage Books, 2002), 154.

[5]Ibid., 160-161.

[6]Peter Calvocoressi, *Top Secret Ultra* (New York: Pantheon Books, 1980), 57.

[7]Ronald Lewin, *Ultra Goes To War* (New York: McGraw-Hill Book Company, 1978), 197.

[8]Antony Beevor, *Crete: The Battle and the Resistance* (London, United Kingdom: John Murray Ltd., 1991), 89-94.

[9]Ralph Bennett, *Ultra and the Mediterranean Strategy* (New York: William Morrow and Company Inc., 1989), 58.

[10]Lewin, 157-159.

[11]Ibid., 71.

[12]Bennett, 57; and Freyberg, 268.

[13]Freyberg, 286.

[14]Ibid., 277-278.

[15]Bennett, 52.

[16]Bennett, 20; and Keegan, 181.

[17]Keegan, 182.

[18]Freyberg was certainly a multinational commander, commanding a diverse group of British and Commonwealth troops in addition to the Greek armed forces on Crete. Freyberg was not a true 'joint' commander however for the operation with RAF and Royal Navy support being commanded separately from Middle East Command. Freyberg was responsible for all troops *on* Crete, therefore should be considered as a ground force commander (or Coalition Forces Land Component Commander in today's terms) rather than a true operational (or Joint Task Force) commander.

[19]Freyberg served under General Sir Claude Auchinleck in North Africa when he was the General Officer Commanding Middle East, and General Mark Clark who commanded the US 5th Army in Italy.

[20]Brigadier-General (later Major-General) Sir Howard Karl Kippenberger (1897-1957) was one of New Zealand's most able brigade commanders during the war, well-respected by his troops and commanders alike. Kippenberger, who failed academically at school, enlisted as an infantryman at the onset of World War I, and served at the Somme. Later that year, as a battalion sniper, Kippenberger was seriously wounded and discharged from the Army. Returning to study law, Kippenberger displayed obvious potential for military command in the Territorial Force, largely owing to his study and grasp of modern warfare. Kippenberger sailed as part of 2 NZEF as commander of the 20th Bn. Commanding the battalion in Greece, Kippenberger was promoted to temporary Colonel to command the ad-hoc 10th NZ Bde on Crete. Kippenberger fought with 20th Bn or as the commander of 5th NZ Bde throughout the next two years in all the major engagements of the 2nd NZ Div. Wounds, capture and battle weariness took its toll on Kippenberger. As the acting commander of 2nd NZ Div at Cassino, Kippenberger was wounded, losing both feet and evacuated. Promoted to major-general at the end of the war, he oversaw the production of twenty-three of the volumes that make up the New Zealand Official History of the Second World War. Knighted in 1948, Kippenberger wrote *Infantry Brigadier*, still seen as a timeless account of infantry tactics and command. Source: Glyn Harper, *Kippenberger, Howard Karl 1897-1957* (Dictionary of New Zealand Biography, updated 7 July 2005); available from http://www.dnzb.govt.nz/; Internet; accessed 25 October 2005.

[21]Laurie Barber and John Tonkin-Covell, *Freyberg: Churchill's Salamander* (London, United Kingdom: Century Hutchinson Ltd., 1990), 2-3.

[22]Geoffrey Cox, *A tale of Two Battles: A Personal Memoir of Crete and the Western Desert 1941* (London, United Kingdom: William Kimber & Co. Ltd., 1987), 55-56; and Freyberg, 270.

[23]Brigadier-General (later Lieutenant-General) Edward Puttick (1890-1976) served in World War I in Samoa, Egypt, and on the Western Front. He commanded 3rd Infantry Bn at Passchendaele and was shot in the lung in 1918. Puttick held a number of staff appointments in New Zealand and England between the wars and upon declaration of war was named as commander 4th NZ Bde, commanding the brigade in the defense and withdrawal during Greece. Puttick was made a temporary Major-General and acting

commander of 2nd NZ Div on Crete when Freyberg assumed command of CREFORCE. Following the battle Puttick was offered the appointment of Chief of General Staff in New Zealand, and was promoted to Lieutenant-General in 1942. Puttick agreed with Fraser that 2 NZEF should remain in the Middle East, and was instrumental in organizing the defensive agreements with the United States to defend the country against the threat of Japanese attack in the Pacific. Source: W. David McIntyre, *Puttick, Edward 1890-1976* (Dictionary of New Zealand Biography, updated 7 July 2005); available from http://www.dnzb.govt.nz/; Internet; accessed 26 October 2005.

[24] Daniel M. Davin, *Official History of New Zealand in the Second World War, 1939-45, Crete* (Wellington, New Zealand: War History Branch, Department of Internal Affairs, 1953), 42; and Freyberg, 270.

[25] Sir John White, interview 7a.

[26] Freyberg, 271-272.

[27] Ibid., 275.

[28] War History Branch New Zealand. *Official History of New Zealand in the Second World War, 1939-45 Documents Relating to New Zealand's Participation in the Second World War 1939-45: Volume I* (Wellington, New Zealand: War History Branch Department of Internal Affairs, 1949), 285-288.

[29] Barber and Tonkin-Covell, 36; and MacDonald, 151-152.

[30] Barber and Tonkin-Covell, 11; and MacDonald 153.

[31] Barber and Tonkin-Covell, 12.

[32] Davin, 27.

[33] Haddon Donald, interviewed by Sergeant Brenton Beach, 19 September 2001, interview 3b, transcript, Queen Elizabeth II Army Memorial Museum Veterans Oral History Project, Waiouru, New Zealand. and Sir John White, interview 7b.

[34] Barber and Tonkin-Covell, 42.

[35] Barber and Tonkin-Covell, 17; and Davin, 56.

[36] Brigadier B. H. Chappel arrived on Crete on 19 March to command 14th Infantry Bde, and assumed by default responsibility for the island's defenses. Chappel handed this over to Weston on 2 April 1941 when the MNBDO was directed to deploy to Crete. Chappel spent the remainder of the operation commanding the 14th Infantry Bde at Heráklion.

[37] Davin, 288.

[38] Brigadier-General (later Major-General) George Alan Vasey (1895-1945) served at the Somme, Messines, Passchendaele and Amiens during World War I. After interwar service in India, he volunteered for service in World War II and commanded 19th Aust Bde in Greece and Crete. After the battle Vasey returned to Australia and, upon promotion, commanded the 7th Div in Papua New Guinea. He was killed in an air crash in 1945 on his way to assume command of the 6th Div at Aitipe. Source: Peter Antill, *Crete 1941: Germany's Lightening Airborne Assault* (Oxford, United Kingdom: 2005), 19-20.

[39] MacDonald, 152.

[40] Brigadier-General Lindsay Merritt Inglis MC (1894-1966) served in the NZEF in Egypt and the Western Front during World War I as an infantry and machine-gun company commander, receiving the Military Cross. Inglis, a lawyer remained in the Territorial Force between wars, initially commanding 27th Machine-Gun Bn, then 4th NZ Bde on Crete. After the battle, Inglis commanded 2nd NZ Div (after Freyberg was wounded) with mixed results at Minqâr Qaim and Ruweisat Ridge in 1942. When Freyberg overlooked Inglis for temporary command of 2nd NZ Div in 1944, preferring Kippenberger, Parkinson or Weir, the insulted Inglis asked to be relieved of command of 4th NZ Bde and returned to New Zealand. Inglis served a President of a Military Government Court in occupied Germany after the war, before returning to New Zealand to become a magistrate. Source: Paul Goldstone, *Inglis, Lindsay Merritt 1894–1966* (Dictionary of New Zealand Biography, updated 7 July 2005); available from http://www.dnzb.govt.nz/; Internet; accessed 30 October 2005.

[41] Davin, 60.

[42] Barber and Tonkin-Covell, 37.

[43] Davin, 68-69.

[44] Brigadier James Hargest MC (1891-1944) took part in the ill-fated Gallipoli campaign in 1915, being seriously wounded. Returning to serve in France, Hargest proved a brave and promising officer, earning the MC and the command of the 2nd Bn, Otago Infantry Regt by war's end. Hargest returned to farming and politics after the war, and after being declared unfit for service due to his World War I wounds, used his political contacts to secure a commission as the commander of 5th NZ Bde. Hargest's Bde conducted a successful delaying action in Greece, and deployed with the majority of the brigade intact to Crete. Hargest was captured in Libya in November 1941 when his headquarters was overrun, but escaped with four other Brigadiers in 1943 from Germany and made his way to England. Hargest was attached as an observer with the British 50th Div for the Normandy invasion, and killed by shellfire in August 1944. Source: J.A.B. Crawford, *Hargest, James 1891-1944* (Dictionary of New Zealand Biography, updated 7 July 2005); available from http://www.dnzb.govt.nz/; Internet; accessed 4 November 2005.

[45] Davin, 62-63.

[46] Ian Stewart, *The Struggle for Crete: 20 May-1 June 1941, A Story of Lost Opportunity* (London, United Kingdom: Oxford University Press, 1966), 129.

[47] Davin, 61.

[48] Barber and Tonkin-Covell, 30.

[49] Lieutenant-Colonel (later Brigadier-General) Leslie Wilton Andrew VC (1897-1969) enlisted as a soldier in 1914, and was awarded a Victoria Cross in 1917 after charging a machine-gun post and defensive positions at La Bassee Ville in France. Remaining in the military after World War I, he rose to the rank of Lieutenant-Colonel and commanded the 22nd Bn at Crete and was positioned at Máleme airfield during the initial airborne attack. Andrew briefly commanded 5th NZ Bde later in 1941 then returned to New Zealand in 1943 to assume area commander appointments as a Brigadier.

[50] Jim H. Henderson, *Official History of New Zealand in the Second World War, 22 Battalion* (Wellington, New Zealand: War History Branch Department of Internal Affairs, 1949), 38.

[51] Davin, 51.

[52] W. G. McClymont, *Official History of New Zealand in the Second World War, 1939-45, To Greece* (Wellington, New Zealand: War History Branch Department of Internal Affairs, 1959), 507-508.

[53] Dave J. C. Pringle and William A. Glue, *Official History of New Zealand in the Second World War, 20 Battalion and Armoured Regiment* (Wellington, New Zealand: War History Branch Department of Internal Affairs, 1949), 98.

[54] Haddon Donald, interview 3b.

[55] Cox, 67.

[56] Ibid., 67.

[57] War History Branch New Zealand, 404.

CHAPTER 5

THE BATTLE

The twelve-day battle that took place on, over and around Crete in late May 1941 has been recounted numerous times. It is not the intent of this thesis to rewrite or recollect the conduct of the entire battle, rather to highlight aspects that are considered relevant to examination of Freyberg's culpability. This chapter will examine key events and decisions made by British and German commanders; most of which occurred within the first three days when the fate of Crete was sealed. Aside from analysis of Freyberg's performance as the operational commander; selected subordinate commanders and their actions will be highlighted from each of the four British defensive sectors to establish whether Freyberg's intent and orders were carried out, and to what level of success. Given the *Luftwaffe* possessed the initiative, at least in the initial stages of the engagement, their actions on 20 May 1941 need to be examined first.

Chapter three examined the operational plan that Student and the XI *Fliegerkorps* staff developed to seize Crete, and the preparatory air attacks that were conducted against the British defenses for the seven days preceding the 20 May 1941 invasion date. On the eve of the invasion, Richthofen's VIII *Fliegerkorps* had isolated the island by driving the Royal Navy from Suda Bay and the Aegean Sea by day, achieved overwhelming thirty to one numerical air superiority over the RAF and, at the height of the preparatory bombardment, launched in excess of 500 sorties against the British troops manning the antiaircraft guns, field defenses and trenches on Crete.[1] On 20 May 1941, soon after 7:00 A.M. the VIII *Fliegerkorps* delivered "one of the most intense local air attacks of the Second World War. . . . According to (Lieutenant) Colonel Andrew (it was) worse than anything he had ever experienced during the artillery bombardments of the First World War"[2] cutting telephone lines, collapsing trenches and limiting any above ground movement by British troops.

The commencement of Operation Merkur Phase Two saw 6, 030[3] parachute and glider-borne troops descend on the Máleme and Suda Sectors before midday on 20 May 1941, intent on seizing the Máleme airfield, Suda Port and Kisamos Kastelli landing area in the west. Capture of these objectives would have allowed reinforcement by air and sea plus the positioning of aircraft at Máleme airfield to support future operations in the east. Once the transport aircraft returned to their Greek bases to refuel and reload, an additional 3,500 troops[4] attacked Retimo and Heráklion. Three critical aspects are evident in the first day from the German perspective.

A 3rd *Fallschirmjäger* Bn operation order captured by the British on 20 May 1941 confirmed that the *Luftwaffe* and OKW underestimated the size of the garrison force on Crete, and their disposition. Many of the parachute drops were conducted close to or onto their objectives (mostly at the airfields and within British battalion boundaries) believing them to be lightly defended, resulting in high casualties through small arms fire. Freyberg estimated that "of more than 7,000 Germans killed on Crete, about half were parachutists, of which the majority were killed on the first day."[5] Included in the casualties on the first day was *Generalmajor* Süssmann, commander of the 7th *Flieger* Div, who died when his glider crashed prior to reaching Crete and *Generalmajor* Meindl, commander of the *Luftlande Sturmregiment* who was wounded and evacuated the next day. By the close of 20 May 1941, the *Luftwaffe* had seized none of the objectives directed in the captured order.[6]

The second evident factor is Student's will to continue to prosecute his original plan without alteration. By midday, the failure of *Gruppe West* to seize Máleme airfield, the defeat of the *Gruppe Mitte* attack on Canea, and the death of Süssmann led *Oberst* Heidrich (now the senior German officer on Crete) to request that troops designated to be dropped that afternoon at Retimo be diverted to reinforce *Gruppe Mitte* at Canea. Student denied the request and looked to *Gruppe Ost* to achieve a lodgment at Heráklion or Retimo, and therefore allow the airlanded deployment of the 5th *Gebirg* Div. Student faced an additional problem at the assembly areas. The *Luftwaffe* staff had optimistically estimated a three-hour turnaround of transport aircraft that could not be achieved due to refueling delays and aircraft losses and damage over the drop zones. As bombers and fighters flew from different airfields, Student was unable to coordinate air support to the Heráklion drop, which he ordered to proceed without close air support.[7] Although still supremely confident, Student's plan appeared to be unraveling on the first day.

Despite the high number of casualties on 20 May 1941, the final factor to be considered, and a telling one on that first day of battle that prevented the *Luftwaffe* forces being totally decimated, was the high quality of the German officers and soldiers conducting the operation. Regardless of losses or separation from their parent unit during the air insertion, both paratroopers and glider troops quickly formed small groups, linked up with other units where they could and pressed the attack. The importance of securing the objectives was apparent at all levels of command, with junior leaders and soldiers realizing their own survival depended on being rapidly reinforced by airlanded troops before enemy counterattacks could be launched. Where lodgments were made relatively free of direct fire or observation such as at the Tavronitis River in the *Gruppe West* sector and the Ayia Valley in *Gruppe Mitte* area, units such as *Generalmajor* Meindl's *Luftlande Sturmregiment* rapidly concentrated and attacked in battalion strength. Backed by overwhelming air support, these attacks not only staved off defeat at the initial point of landing, and repelled local counterattacks, but also achieved limited success in seizing terrain that would affect the conduct of the battle the next day. While Student's operational plan was faltering, it was not due to the lack of commitment or professionalism of his soldiers at the tactical level.

In the Máleme Sector, 5th NZ Bde received the brunt of the morning invasion, and initially had spectacular success. The *Sturmregiment* detachment of seventy-two men tasked to seize Kisamos Kastelli was defeated by the 1st Greek Regt defending the sea-landing site.[8] Landings east of Máleme Airfield fell directly into the 21st, 22nd and 28th (Maori) Bn areas. By midday, both 22nd Bn and 23rd Bn reported to Hargest at HQ 5th NZ Bde that they had cleared and secured their areas and were in a position to counterattack to support 22nd Bn if required. This included having conducted further reconnaissance of the 23rd Bn counterattack route and, although no communications existed between the battalions (there were insufficient wireless sets and landlines had been cut by the preparatory bombardment), had positioned signalers to watch for emergency flares and flags; the 22nd Bn signal to counterattack.[9]

Within the 22nd Bn perimeter, however, a different battle was fought. The dispersed parachute and glider landings relegated much of the fighting to platoon and company level battles. Lacking internal communications to his companies, Andrew was forced to rely on runners from his headquarters to his subordinate commanders. Whilst the battalion successfully accounted for enemy within the perimeter, Andrew was unable to directly engage the Germans west of the Tavronitis River. This area was used by the enemy to assemble and launch attacks against Hill 107, the feature that dominated the 22nd Bn position at Máleme, and other sectors of the defense. Andrew, his perimeter penetrated at times up to five places to his Bn HQ, requested Hargest to launch a counterattack at 2:55 P.M. to relieve pressure on D Coy in the vicinity of the Tavronitis River. Hargest refused, citing the paratrooper threat in 23rd Bn's area precluded them from redeploying. After a local counterattack from Andrew's small infantry and tank reserve failed at 3:30 P.M., Andrew fired his emergency flares, which were not seen by 23rd Bn observers. Toward 5:00 P.M., he again asked Hargest for assistance or he would be forced to withdraw, at which time Hargest replied "well, if you must, you must."[10] After a moment of reflection, however, it is clear that Hargest reconsidered the position of 22nd Bn, and directed a company each from 23rd and 28th Bns reinforce 22nd Bn at Máleme due to arrive at 9:45 P.M.[11]

The lack of urgency to launch the 5th Bde counterattack, and in any significant strength, underlines Hargest's misplaced optimism and failure to appreciate the developing tactical situation. Despite the failed 22nd Bn counterattack and the possibility of the battalion withdrawal from the vital ground for the entire defense of Crete, Hargest reported to 2nd NZ Div at 9:45 P.M. that the situation was "quite satisfactory". Hargest was confident that the two companies he had dispatched to Máleme would be sufficient combat power to reinforce Andrew, but failed to grasp that a counterattack to defeat the Germans was required, not just the reinforcement of the defense. Not reported to HQ 2nd NZ Div was that 22nd Bn was considering withdrawing from Hill 107 and essentially abandoning the airfield, a fact that would have raised alarm at both Puttick's HQ 2nd NZ Div and Freyberg's HQ CREFORCE.[12]

Andrew, out of touch with his subordinate commanders, was unable (or unwilling) to move forward to determine the exact disposition and status of his companies. Additionally, he misread the strength of the German attacks that were after dusk, faltering without the overwhelming air support daylight guaranteed. Accordingly, fearing his forward companies had been cut off and destroyed, and with no sight of reinforcement or counterattack by 5th NZ Bde, Andrew ordered the withdrawal of 22nd Bn under the cover of darkness. Andrew planned to reoccupy Hill 107 once the reinforcements arrived, and did so when the company from 23rd Bn arrived at 10:00 P.M. with only light casualties. The company from the 28th (Maori) Bn however, was contacted by the Germans near the airfield and, unable to locate Andrew, subsequently withdrew. Andrew, fearing that forces left on Hill 107 would be surrounded by first light and unable to hold the terrain when *Luftwaffe* air support commenced, ordered all troops to fall back to the 23rd Bn lines.[13]

Hargest, who had gone to bed that night confident of success at Máleme, was surprised to learn at 4:00 A.M. the next morning of 22nd Bn's complete withdrawal. Between the failed 22nd Bn counterattack and first light on 22 May 1941, there existed a number of opportunities for 5th NZ Bde to counterattack, as directed by Freyberg in orders, to ensure Máleme was held. Hargest must take responsibility for this failure. The positioning of his headquarters in Plantanias was too far removed from his forward three battalions, and his failure to move forward himself left him isolated and unable to make timely decisions. Knowing his communications would be disrupted, Hargest should have placed himself in a position where he could affect the battle.[14] Stewart in *The Struggle for Crete: 20 May-1 June 1941, A Story of Lost Opportunity* sums up opportunity missed by Hargest and 5th NZ Bde:

> Thus on the evening of 20 May the mass of the New Zealand 5th Brigade, including more than 1,600 unwounded infantry, the core of the New Zealand Division, were allowed to settle for the night in misguided and short-lived tranquility. Scattered amongst them, hunted, thirsty, and exhausted, a few dozen surviving Germans crouched in such cover as they could find while a bare two miles to the east, pinned upon the outskirts of the vital airfield, the men of the 22nd Battalion were locked in a death grip with an enemy scarcely more numerous, and considerably more wearier than themselves.[15]

Hargest is also a good example of a commander that had gained his experience in the World War I trench warfare of the battlefields of the Somme and Passchendaele. He failed to grasp the speed at which modern battle developed, especially the new type of warfare involving an airborne element, and therefore the requirement for quick, decisive counterattack to deny lodgment. Knowing that the only opportunity to counterattack free from interference from the *Luftwaffe* fighters and bombers was at night, Hargest should have pushed the counterattack to be complete before first light. Instead, he chose to utilize the remaining hours of darkness to consolidate his brigade in defensive positions east of Máleme. The airfield at Máleme, while still under British indirect fire, was not defended by any formed unit or positions that could provide direct fires against reinforcing aircraft.

The *Gruppe Mitte* assaults into the Canea/Suda Sector sought to not only seize Canea and Suda Port but also to eliminate the garrison headquarters, and therefore the coordinated defense of the island. As with the Máleme Sector, parachute and glider troops met stiff resistance from 10th NZ Bde and 4th NZ Bde west and south of Canea. In the 10th NZ Bde sector, Kippenberger immediately had to consolidate his defense as companies and platoons of the two Greek battalions (the 6th Bn and the 8th Bn) in the Ayia Valley were killed or abandoned their positions and withdrew. For the remainder of the morning, Kippenberger's 10th Composite Bn, Division Petrol Company and Divisional Cavalry employed as infantry conducted a series of local counterattacks and delaying actions to deny penetration to Canea from the Ayia Valley. Kippenberger commanded from the heart of his small brigade, and although the enemy gained a foothold in the Ayia Valley similar to that at the Tavronitis River at Máleme, Kippenberger felt a counterattack of sufficient force would clear the remaining German troops from the valley. Kippenberger's greatest concern was the number of troops he was losing to fighters and bombers overhead, and the hard-won terrain he gained by counterattacking was soon lost as British troops were then bombed out of their positions.[16]

The adjacent areas to the east of 10th NZ Bde occupied by 4th NZ Bde and the MNBDO all were engaged in that first morning to differing levels of intensity. The 2nd/8th Aust Bn at Geogioupolis was moved to Suda Sector to assist Weston deny penetration in the MNBDO area, and 4th NZ Bde (especially the 18th Bn and the 19th Bn) all contained the enemy within their sectors conducting local counterattacks within battalion areas. The heavy fighting in the Ayia Valley area quickly identified it as the most likely enemy area of concentration, and Kippenberger requested to 2nd NZ Div an immediate counterattack be undertaken on the afternoon of 20 May 1941.

A counterattack into the Ayia valley was well within the capabilities of 2nd NZ Div. At 11:00 A.M. Freyberg had released 4th NZ Bde, less the Welch Regt, from its reserve tasking to the control of Puttick's 2nd NZ Div for the purpose of conducting counterattacks within the division's area of operations either to support 4th NZ Bde, 5th NZ Bde or 10th NZ Bde. Considerable operational risk was taken by Freyberg in this decisive action, leaving only one battalion as the CREFORCE reserve, and at the time no reported contact with the enemy at Retimo or Heráklion and the threat of a seaborne landing still to be considered. The boldness of this move so early in the battle confirms Freyberg's intent to immediately counterattack any enemy action before it could decisively develop further.[17]

Although Puttick was aware of the building threat in the Ayia Valley, Kippenberger had to again request the counterattack be launched at 2:15 P.M. Davin argues in the *New Zealand Official History of the Second World War* that Puttick believed this action to be only a secondary action to the developing Máleme action. In addition, to commit to a counterattack in the Valley in strength by daylight would risk the reserve being defeated by air and ground forces, and would not leave sufficient combat power to support Hargest's 5th NZ Bde if required. The fact that Hargest had reported a satisfactory situation to Puttick did not convince him to launch a 4th NZ Bde attack to support Kippenberger.[18] Puttick, it could be argued, suffered from the same indecision as Hargest, made worse by a lack of accurate information and intermittent communications between units. Only when Kippenberger reported at 5:30 P.M. (falsely it turned out) the preparation of a possible landing area in the Ayia Valley did Puttick act.

Despite having three battalions available with which to counterattack (the 18th, 19th and 20th Bns) Puttick chose to only direct 4th NZ Bde to attack as follows:

> 10 Bde reports construction of landing ground in PRISON (Ayia) AREA 9553. 4 Inf Bde will counterattack with one Bn, Lt tks and carriers to clear prison area of

enemy. When attack completed 19 Bn will come under comd 10 Bde to hold posn on left of 1 COMP on line previously held by 6 Gk Bn.[19]

Inglis also was cautious, believing that he should retain the majority of 4th NZ Bde for a possible brigade-sized counterattack the next day, and that the attack into Ayia valley should not detract from either future operations or the current defense. Accordingly he issued an order for 19th Bn to attack with the "Bn if the situation permits, two Coys if Bn Comd considers that one Coy should be left in present posn."[20] Major Blackburn, the Commanding Officer of the 19th Bn, given his current defensive disposition, attacked with two companies, the mortar platoon, and the Bn HQ supported by the 3rd Hussars.

With no communications or contact to Kippenberger prior to the attack, Blackburn's troops advanced immediately on a separate axis from the tanks towards the enemy. After the companies had departed, Blackburn was able to find Kippenberger, who identified that the counterattack force was too weak to overcome the enemy in the Ayia Valley and directed it be cancelled. This is an accurate assessment from Kippenberger given that the better part of three battalions from *Gruppe Mitte* had landed in the Ayia Valley area, and had concentrated on areas of seized terrain in up to battalion strength. Kippenberger's 10th NZ Bde was able to hold existing defensive positions on the night of 20 May 1941 and it contained the potential penetration between the New Zealand forward brigades. However, Freyberg's other subordinate New Zealand commanders had failed to counterattack with speed and sufficient force to not only retake key terrain, but also more importantly to defeat *Gruppes West* and *Mitte* before they could consolidate.

Brigadier Vasey's only action in the battle to date in the Retimo Sector had been committing an infantry battalion to reinforce Weston's Suda Sector during the first airborne wave. The attack on Retimo was conducted by the remainder of *Gruppe Mitte*, consisting two parachute battalions of the 2nd *Fallschirmjäger* Regt reinforced with machine-gun companies and artillery batteries, under the command of *Oberst* Strum. Although preceded by heavy bombardment from Richthofen's VIII *Fliegerkorps*, poor intelligence on enemy defensive strengths and dispositions, coupled with an uncoordinated parachute drop directly onto Lieutenant-Colonel Ian Campbell's defenses at Retimo, caused initially heavy losses.[21]

Heavy fighting ensued for the remainder of the day and early evening, with Campbell immediately counterattacking twice across the airfield to push Sturm back to the hills surrounding the airfield, and the Greek Police holding at the town of Retimo. Campbell lost both of his tanks in these attacks, and although he held his defensive line, had to relinquish Hill A that overlooked the airfield. After bitter hand-to-hand fighting throughout the day, Strum dug in on the ground won and awaited daylight and the return of the *Luftwaffe* to press the attack. The 2nd /11th Aust Bn, who buried 400 enemy dead on 21 May 1941 in their battalion sector alone, was a measure the strength of the initial defense at Retimo. Campbell planned two counterattacks for the morning of 21 May 1941 to retake Hill A while Sturm, his regimental signals unit killed in the initial landing, was unable to advise Student of their failure to seize their objective. Student would remain out of touch with the 2nd *Fallschirmjäger* Regt for the next two days as Sturm and Campbell's forces fought to a standstill.[22]

The dislocated *Luftwaffe* attack at Retimo was repeated at Heráklion that same afternoon. *Gruppe Ost*, the reinforced 1st *Fallschirmjäger* Regt under *Oberst* Bräuer, was unable to coordinate the fighter, bomber and transport aircraft arrival over the drop zone:

> The formations started in incorrect tactical sequence, and arrived over their target areas between sixteen and nineteen hundred hours not closed up but in successive formation and at the most by squadrons. The bulk of the forces had to land without fighter protection. Moreover, in the end, the force delivered was some six hundred men less than had been intended.[23]

The drop over the landing zone without fighter support allowed Brigadier Brian Chappel's well-concealed antiaircraft guns and troops occupying defensive positions to fire mercilessly on the unprotected transport aircraft. Bräuer who landed unopposed away from the airfield thought, again through poor intelligence, that it had been taken by the initial assault, and informed Student that Heráklion was open. This optimism was poor judgement and short-lived as the two battalions tasked to converge on the objective were driven back by an immediate infantry and armor counterattack by Chappel's forces, suffering over 300 dead and 100 wounded in the 2nd Bn in the first thirty minutes alone.[24] The failure of 1st *Fallschirmjäger* Regt to seize the town of Heráklion in the face of stiff Cretan resistance; the failure to drop essentially a battalions worth of infantry, and the rapid and decisive counterattack by Chappel meant that Bräuer failed to achieve any of his tactical objectives by day's end. Bräuer's only success was the unopposed landing further west of Heráklion to cut the Retimo-Heráklion Road and prevent any possible reinforcement from the west.

Freyberg, his communications with subordinate commands intermittent throughout the day, by late on 20 May 1941, was cautious in his assessment of the day's fighting in a cable to Wavell:

> Today has been a hard one. We have been hard pressed. I believe that so far we hold the airfields at Máleme, Heráklion and Retimo and the two harbours. The margin by which we hold them is a bare one and it would be wrong of me to paint an optimistic picture. The fighting has been heavy and large numbers of Germans have been killed. Communications are most difficult. The scale of air attack upon

us has been severe. Everybody here realises the vital issue and we will fight it out.[25]

The lack of intelligence gained by the *Luftwaffe* prior to the invasion, especially the troop dispositions and location of antiaircraft guns at the majority of the defensive sites, is testimony to Freyberg's ability to conceal his defensive preparations, and the fire and movement discipline of the troops on Crete. Some poor fire control did occur, notably at Máleme by the MNBDO antiaircraft detachment that quickly gained the attention of the *Luftwaffe*, where as positions that held their fire initially against the fighters were able to wreak havoc against the transport aircraft over the drop zones.

The majority of the drop zones chosen by the *Luftwaffe* on 20 May 1941 were as Freyberg had anticipated based upon Ultra and his own appreciation. The deficiencies of Freyberg's defensive disposition in not adequately defending the Tavronitis River and head of the Ayia Valley is an easy target for historians as *that is where the enemy landed*. Had the *Luftwaffe* concentrated its airborne and glider-borne operations in an undefended area elsewhere, it is likely the same conclusion that Freyberg failed to secure all landing zones could be made. The success of Chappel and Campbell on the afternoon of 20 May 1941, when the *Luftwaffe* was unable synchronize its bomber, fighter and transport aircraft over the targets, also is cruel in analyzing the defense for the troops fighting at Máleme and Canea. Had the initial attack been as fractured as in the afternoon, Hargest, Puttick and Inglis may have had the opportunity and decisiveness, free from coordinated fighter and bomber attack, to immediately press the counterattack as Freyberg had directed, and as Kippenberger, Chappel and Campbell had done so. Additionally, had the counterattack in the Tavronitis River area been conducted in strength and quickly on 20 May 1941, the flaw in Freyberg's planned defensive layout would have become a benefit.

Holding the high ground that surrounded the Tavronitis River, the defenders would have been able to dominate the lower ground with direct and observed indirect fire to support the counterattack force and defeat the lodgment.

For Student, in Athens, the failure to secure a lodgment on the first day appeared to spell the failure of his plan, and the first likely operational defeat of German ground forces in the war. Ironically, luck was kind to Student at the end of the day on 20 May 1941, when the 600 paratroopers of *Gruppe Ost* were unable to be transported to Heráklion due to a lack of coordination and aircraft. These, along with remaining 7th *Flieger* Div soldiers at the bases in Greece, provided Student with the operational reserve that he had not early included in his plan, but now desperately needed. Overnight, Student directed two events that changed the conduct of the invasion:

> During the night I sent for Captain Kleye, a bold go-getting character on my staff, and told him to take a Junkers 52 and land at Máleme in order to get a personal feeling of how things were going with the Sturm Regiment. . . . He managed to land on the airfield and also to get off again although fired at by the enemy. In this way he was able to bring back the important information that the western edge of the airstrip lay in dead ground.[26]

With Máleme confirmed as the area most likely to bring success, Student focused his resources onto exploiting the lodgment gained, regardless of the fact that Máleme airfield was still under fire. Along with both VIII and XI *Fliegerkorps* concentrating on reinforcing *Gruppe West*, Student directed the 1st Motor Sailing Flotilla, complete with heavy weapons and a battalion of the 5th *Gebirg* Div, to arrive at Máleme by last light on 21 May 1941 and a further battalion to prepare to airland immediately in the area west of Máleme.

The relentless reinforcement of Máleme that followed by Student's troops is best described by Freyberg:

> We had made a miscalculation. It had not been considered feasible for aircraft to land in the riverbed west of the Máleme airfield. But during the morning troop carriers began to crash-land there, and also on the beaches west of the airfield. These landings continued under constant shellfire from nine field guns and despite this observed artillery fire, which destroyed numbers of the enemy planes, it went on regardless of loss to machines or life. The enemy were prepared to lose any number of planes, for those which were wrecked in landing or from fire were simply dragged off the landing ground to make more room for more to land where these had been destroyed.[27]

Student's parachute reserve had mixed success. Two companies dropped to the west of Máleme succeeded in linking up with and reinforcing the *Sturmregiment* occupying the vital ground at Hill 107; however, two further companies landed in the 28th (Maori) Bn area at Plantanias and were decimated. With Máleme airfield physically occupied by the Germans, yet under constant fire, reinforcements poured in to secure the lodgment and prepared for the inevitable counterattack once darkness fell and *Luftwaffe* air support returned to their bases in Greece.

For 5th NZ Bde, by first light on the morning of 21 May 1941, the opportunity to counterattack Máleme had passed. Andrew, Allen and Leckie had discussed the possibility at the 23rd Bn HQ of using 21st Bn and 23rd Bn to retake Hill 107 while the depleted 22nd Bn held the current defensive line. However, without consent or direction from Hargest, again out of communications, they were reluctant to commit to the attack. The positioning of Hargest's headquarters far to the rear at Plantanias, again slowed the decision making process, and Hargest did not either come forward to his line battalions or retain sufficient communications with which to effectively command the defense. Hargest, based upon the scant information received from his battalion commanders, and lacking battlefield awareness, agreed to holding the defensive line as opposed to counterattacking. At first light, HQ 2nd NZ Div and HQ CREFORCE were informed of the withdrawal of 22nd Bn, and that 5th NZ Bde no longer held the Máleme airfield.[28]

Freyberg informed of the tactical situation by landline at first light on 21 May 1941, and during a visit forward to HQ 2nd NZ Div, convened a meeting consisting Puttick, Inglis, Vasey and Stewart[29] to discuss the conduct of a counterattack to retake Máleme. Hargest, not attending the orders group, had recommended to Puttick that the counterattack be conducted under the cover of darkness only, owing to the intensity of air attack that prevented the movement of troops by day. Having supported the initial airborne invasion, Richthofen's VIII *Fliegerkorps* was now engaged in its secondary task; preventing reinforcement at the Máleme lodgment by bombing and strafing British lines of communication and reinforcement. Although waiting until darkness to commence the attack would result in a greater number of Germans defending the Airfield, all commanders including Freyberg agreed that to attack by day would result in too many casualties, of both men and the limited amount of armor that was available.

Freyberg had one other aspect of the German invasion to take into consideration at this stage; the seaborne invasion. From Ultra Signals OL 2170 and OL 2/302 (see appendix E) he expected on the second day of the operation the seaborne landings to commence. The crippling losses Cunningham's fleet had taken in the battle so far did not give Freyberg confidence that, in the face of such overwhelming air superiority and unable to operate close to Crete by day, the Royal Navy would be able to defeat a German seaborne attack. Additional to this intelligence, and the previous day's action of the unsuccessful *Sturmregiment* to seize the Kisamos Kastelli landing site, he received a further OL Signal 15/389:

> On continuation of attack Colorado (Crete), reliably reported that among operations planned for Twenty-first May is air landing two mountain battalions and attack Canea. Landing from echelon of small ships depending of situation at sea.[30]

Beevor, in his book *Crete: The Battle and the Resistance* contends that Freyberg misread this signal, and thought a seaborne attack on Canea (not Máleme or elsewhere) was imminent, and therefore retained an excessive amount of troops to defend against this eventuality rather than commit sufficient forces to the counterattack to seize Máleme.[31] Davin in the *Official History of New Zealand in the Second World War* cites that, additional to the 2nd NZ Div that had been continually engaged over the past twenty-four hours, there were a number of other units in the Canea and Suda Bay area that could have been allocated. A reorganization of units to ensure that coastal defense was maintained, would have freed infantry units such as the 1st Welch or 2nd/8th Aust Bn from their defensive positions guarding against the seaborne invasion. Davin goes on to state three reasons why this did not occur. At the conference, Puttick advised that two fresh battalions, not currently committed to fighting, would be sufficient to conduct the counterattack. From 5th NZ Bde the 28th (Maori) Bn was chosen as it had not been involved in the heaviest of the Máleme Sector fighting, and 20th Bn from 4th NZ Bde. Secondly, most of the units in the Canea/Suda Bay were ancillary units and lacked many, if any, weapons, transport or communications. Lastly, Freyberg did not possess the staff with which to effect such a complex reorganization of the defenses in time to contribute further forces to the counterattack.[32]

Additional to the two infantry battalions, Freyberg allocated a troop of light tanks, and an artillery battery, and requested air support from GHQ Middle East to bomb the airfield between midnight and 2:00 A.M.[33] Two flaws in the counterattack plan were evident from its conception. Firstly, in order for 20th Bn to conduct the attack it had to be released from its current defensive task defending against a seaborne landing in the Canea area. To do so, Freyberg directed Brigadier Vasey to move his 2nd/7th Aust Bn to cover the 20th Bn positions in time for it to reach the start line at the Plantanias River by 1:00 A.M. on 22 May 1941. If either battalion were late, then the attack would not be complete by first light and the return of the *Luftwaffe*.

Secondly, neither Freyberg nor Puttick designated who was to be in overall command of the attack. A two-battalion attack with supporting arms should have been commanded by one of the brigade headquarters in CREFORCE, especially as the battalions came from different brigades, albeit the same division. Within 2nd NZ Div there were two options; either HQ 4th NZ Bde under Inglis as the designated CREFORCE reserve commander conduct the attack; or HQ 5th NZ Bde as the parent headquarters of the 28th (Maori) Bn under Hargest who was best placed to coordinate the movement of the battalions through his own brigade area. Both Freyberg and Puttick were responsible for this coordination, although Puttick should have made this decision as all of the subordinate commanders were from his division. Freyberg, having relinquished command of the division prior to the battle, had faith in his subordinate commanders and tried not to meddle below his command level, however in this instance could have ensured a more robust chain of command than that which developed.[34] It fell to Hargest to command the counterattack force once it arrived at the Plantanias River start-line, and HQ 5th NZ Bde subsequently issued the following order for the attack:

1. Starting Time for Advance   0100 hrs   22 May 41
2. Starting Time for Attack   0400 hrs   22 May 41
3. Line of Advance: 20 Bn on the right of rd, but when past MÁLEME CEMETERY and on to AIRFIELD, the left of the Bn will move under the terrace, 100 yds left of the rd.
4. 28 Bn to move to left of rd, and when nearing objective will make certain its left is on top of KAVKAZIA Hill (107).
5. On completion of task, 20 Bn will move back to ridge in front MÁLEME VILLAGE with posts thrust forward to command the AIRFIELD. Thence approximately along line of rd to Pt 107.
6. 28 Bn as soon as task is finished and it has handed over to 20 Bn will withdraw to its location at PLANTANIAS by covered routes.
7. 21 Bn will occupy a line from Pt 107 back to wireless station.
8. Bde Report Centre at Old Bde HQ PLANTANIAS VILLAGE.

Headquarters   W.W. MASON Lt
5 Inf Bde   Lieut.
FIELD   S.C.
21 May 41   5 Inf Bde[35]

Hargest's order, again demonstrates his failure to understand the importance of not only clearing the Germans from the airfield, but also to take and dominate the terrain surrounding the Máleme, thus defeating the German lodgment. His order sought to retake only what terrain had been lost previously and did not utilize the resources available to strengthen the defense.[36] If the 20th Bn and 28th (Maori) Bn were successful in seizing the objectives of Hill 107 and the airfield, then Hargest could have used the remaining three battalions of his brigade to exploit past the airfield and seize the Tavronitis River area.

As units were maneuvering after dusk to prepare for the counterattack, the two German seaborne convoys carrying a *Gebirgs* Bn each plus antiaircraft batteries, tanks, heavy weapons and ammunition approached Crete. The convoys were not in the strength Freyberg had envisaged, but they still posed a serious threat to the defense of Crete if they could be landed in areas to either reinforce a decisive attack at Máleme or Canea, or drive a penetration on the coastal road in between Freyberg's dispersed and isolated units. Cunningham, forewarned of their movement, had returned to the Aegean Sea after having to move south earlier in the day to escape a heavy *Luftwaffe* attack that sunk the destroyer *Juno* and severely damaged the cruiser *Ajax*. Just before midnight, Cunningham's naval forces discovered the 1st Motor Sailing Flotilla north of Canea and all vessels, less a single caique and the Italian torpedo boat *Lupo*, which was severely damaged, were sunk. The one remaining caique was sunk on the morning of 22 May 1941 near Heráklion. Upon learning of the destruction of the 1st Flotilla, *Generaladmiral* Schüster was forced order the 2nd Flotilla to return to Piraeus.[37]

Cunningham was to pay for his boldness in staying in the Aegean by day on 22 May 1941. After sighting and engaging the 2nd Flotilla, Admiral King's Force C, which was positioned to the northeast screening against possible Italian naval support to the battle, came under severe air attack. By the end of the day, Cunningham's Mediterranean Fleet lost two cruisers and one destroyer, and had a further two battleships, two cruisers and several destroyers damaged.[38] Although they had succeeded in preventing Crete from being reinforced, the heavy losses Cunningham received on 22 May 1941 severely degraded his ability to guard, replenish, and support Freyberg for the remainder of the operation. This included not being in a position to provide naval gunfire support to the defending ground troops, who, in the absence of air cover and possessing minimal artillery pieces, were unable to effectively engage German positions outside of direct fire range.

The relief-in-place of the 20th Bn by 2nd/7th Aust Bn was due to be completed in the 4th NZ Bde area of operations by 10:00 P.M. on 21 May 1941. Although 2nd/7th

Aust Bn departed Geogioupolis on time, the battalion received intense *Luftwaffe* bombing and strafing alone the route delaying it by three hours. Therefore, 20th Bn was only released from its defensive position at 1:00 A.M. 22 May 1941, the time it was supposed to be commencing the advance from Plantanias. Inglis requested from Puttick that the battalion be released prior to the arrival of 2nd/7th Aust Bn, but both Puttick and Freyberg denied the request.[39] At the time of the request, the sea battle was raging in front of Canea. Although not stated, this possibly contributed to both commander's reluctance to weaken the defensive line at the most likely point and time of a seaborne attack. Additionally, both 4th NZ Bde and 10th NZ Bde were under sporadic attack from last light on 21 May 1941 within their own areas, and this prevented a closer 2nd NZ Div battalion being ordered to assume the defensive responsibility of 20th Bn.

Hargest upon meeting the 20th Bn and 28th (Maori) Bn commanders (Lieutenant-Colonel James Burrows and Lieutenant-Colonel G. Dittmer respectively) at Plantanias at approximately 2:45 A.M. found that not all of Burrows' rifle companies had yet arrived at the start-line. Hargest sought approval from Puttick to cancel the attack owing to the delays and the missing troops, but was ordered to continue. At 3:30 A.M., the two battalions commenced the attack along the coast toward Máleme airfield. The 21st Bn and 23rd Bn conducted supporting attacks to extend the defensive line west from their current position and in an attempt to retake Hill 107. Hargest's plan lacked sufficient coordination to ensure these two battalions fought as part of the counterattack force relegating them to conducting independent battalion missions. That Hargest failed to personally lead the counterattack, in essence involving four infantry battalions, in his brigade area of operations is both incomprehensible and inexcusable.

By 8:00 A.M. on 22 May 1941, both battalions in the counterattack had fought through the initial line of German defenses conducted in a series of strong points on the coastal road. The 28th (Maori) Bn was engaged in house to house fighting at the town of Pirgos, one mile to the east of the Airfield, and while elements of the 20th Bn made it to the edge of the airfield, they could not hold the ground under the resumption of air attacks after first light. Although initially successful also in 21st Bn's area, lacking air support, artillery, armor and coordination with the counterattack force, these attacks were driven off by the Germans by last light on 22 May 1941.[40] Freyberg himself summed up the counterattack:

> Our counterattack to recapture the airfield with only two battalions of Infantry went in too late, and was badly planned. The weak Artillery support did not help, and the Air Force never turned up. The men did get a footing on the airfield, but after dawn on 22 May, the Luftwaffe came over and our forward troops were again heavily bombed, and were driven back. No movement in the forward areas was possible by daylight, and by the night of 22/23 the Germans had reinforced Máleme from Greece, and it was too late.[41]

The counterattack continued throughout the day of 22 May 1941, with poor communications from the forward battalions to Hargest's headquarters contributing to the confusion. Two messages from HQ 5th NZ Bde to HQ 2nd NZ Div demonstrated how out of touch Hargest was with the tactical situation at Máleme:

> 11:50 A.M. Reliable reports state airfield occupied by own troops line now held EAST side of drome.
> 1:25 P.M. Recent message makes position confused. M (the Brigade Major) going to investigate. Tps NOT so far forward on left as believed. Officers on ground believe enemy preparing for attack and take serious view. I disagree but of course they have closer view. Will visit your HQ when M returns.[42]

The failure of Hargest to counterattack immediately on 20 May 1941 and his poor coordination of the 5th NZ Bde counterattack on the night of 21 May 1941, coupled with tactical lethargy shown at times by Puttick and Inglis during the first two days, highlight a fear Freyberg had prior to the war. New Zealand had reduced its interwar army to a bare minimum training force. The lack of experienced commanders in the New Zealand Army in 1939 that forced Fraser to seek an experienced officer outside of the country to command 2NZEF, and ultimately Freyberg's appointment, was evident at the subordinate brigade and battalion levels. The brigade commanders were all selected by the government on recommendation of the Army Chief of Staff. Hargest, himself, had secured his appointment through his political connections. Most of the battalion commanders, many of whom had served gallantly in World War I (and were highly decorated), held only junior officer appointments in that war, or served in the reserves leading up to World War II. All battalion and brigade commanders were at least over the age of forty (Hargest was fifty), a concern that Freyberg later commented on:

> I should also have realised that some of my Commanders, men from World War I, were to old for the hand-to-hand fighting, and were not likely to stand up to the strain of an all out battle of the nature that eventually developed around Máleme Airfield and its eastern approaches. I should have replaced the old age group with younger men who, as a rule, although less experienced as fighting soldiers, stood up much better to the physical and mental strain of a long and bitter series of battles.[43]

The same criticism of Hargest, Inglis and Puttick has also been leveled at Freyberg for the first two days of the battle by some historians. However, it is arguable that many fail to view Freyberg as the operational commander, and judge him only in relation to the conduct of the New Zealand division in Crete. This is poor analysis of the responsibilities of this level of command. Freyberg was responsible (as essentially an operational-level corps commander), in today's terminology, of planning two levels down (brigade), and directing tasks to his subordinate commanders one level down (division). Therefore, in relation to 2nd NZ Div, Freyberg's allocation of sufficient resources from the operational level (the release of the CREFORCE reserve on both 20 May and 21 May 1941 with additional armored and artillery support are examples) to Puttick to conduct two brigade-sized counterattacks at the tactical level is the correct response. Mindful that Freyberg only possessed an ad-hoc staff, he was also responsible for securing whatever air support to the defense and the counterattacks he could from Middle East Command (which he requested but never materialized) and coordinating with Cunningham the naval support and replenishment to the operation. This was especially important once the ground lines of communication were severed between Canea and Retimo on 21 May 1941, and Retimo and Heráklion on 22 May 1941, and replenishment was only available to these units by sea.

Freyberg's direction of these tactical tasks was correct; however, with communications so intermittent below brigade level, once resources had been committed to the task, he had no means of personally influencing the tactical fight. Freyberg often moved between CREFORCE HQ and the headquarters of 2nd NZ Div and MNBDO on the first two days to gauge the level of fighting. However, not possessing sufficient and reliable wireless communications, such action placed him out of contact for long periods with the remainder of the CREFORCE units, and both Cunningham and Wavell at the strategic and operational level, whose support the defense of Crete relied upon. Freyberg would later write that "he ought to have gone forward and personally led the counterattack on the second night",[44] and although this is an admirable gesture, this would be akin to a modern battalion commander leading a platoon attack.

Máleme became by 22 May 1941, the operational focus for both the Allies and the German forces on Crete. At Heráklion, "by the evening of 22 May, 1,450 of the 2,000 parachutists who had been dropped . . . were dead, at a cost of only 50 British and Australian casualties. The 600 Germans that remained were scattered . . . and for the time being posing no threat to the well-established garrison."[45] At Retimo, Campbell conducted two successful counterattacks to retake Hill A on the morning of 22 May 1941 and captured Strum, the German regimental commander. As at Heráklion, the lines of communication to the remainder of the force were cut, but both brigades were able to reestablish control of their defensive positions and report to Freyberg that they were holding, albeit under increasing *Luftwaffe* air attack.

Some criticism after the battle was leveled at Chappel for not advancing from Heráklion west along the coastal road to link up with Campbell and then continue to Canea to assist 2nd NZ Div, and cite that although decisive on the first day, that Chappel lacked urgency and imagination thereafter. A number of factors influenced Chappel's decision not to advance from Heráklion. Firstly, he was not ordered by Freyberg to do so; he was still responsible for the defense of Heráklion Airfield and would have had to leave behind a sizable force to conduct this task. Secondly, he possessed neither sufficient ammunition nor transport to conduct such a move. Lastly, the state of the road and German activity on it (and above it after the *Luftwaffe* had established a forward base at Máleme) prevented it. Chappel was able, however, to move some light tanks and field guns to Suda by lighter once Heráklion was secure. Unfortunately, this was too late to assist, other than in the conduct of the withdrawal.[46]

The failed counterattack on Máleme allowed the reinforcement by the 5th *Gebirgs* Div to continue into the airfield, albeit under heavy indirect fire, on 22 May 1941. "By the end of the day, Máleme had become a vast aircraft graveyard with 137 wrecks littering the perimeter."[47] For Student, the failure to secure a lodgment on 21 May 1941, the high number of aircraft losses and casualties, and the growing list of additional resources required for the Crete operation, was telling. An OKW meeting on 22 May 1941 conceded that assistance from the Italian Navy was required to draw the Royal Navy away from Crete, and that the operation must be concluded rapidly in order to free Richthofen's VIII *Fliegerkorps* to prepare for Operation Barbarossa. Student, who was about to fly to Crete to assume command of the ground operation, was unceremoniously ordered by Göring to remain in Greece, and Ringel replaced him as the operational commander. Although not relieved as commander of XI *Fliegerkorps*, Student paid for the lack of immediate success that he promised Göring, Löhr and Hitler the airborne troops could deliver.[48]

Informed of the failed counterattack on 22 May 1941, Freyberg's immediate response was to conduct another attack on the night of 22 May 1941. With the immediate seaborne threat defeated, and both Vasey and Chappel's brigades involved in heavy fighting but still secure in their positions at Retimo and Heráklion, Freyberg again sought to defeat the lodgment at Máleme:

> The vital question was whether we could attack and dislodge the enemy from the Máleme Airfield area. . . . The enemy had absolute air superiority; not only could he bomb any movement but he could call upon about 400 fighter ground-strafers with cannon guns which would, and in fact did, prevent any movement during the hours of daylight. We had counterattacked by night and succeeded, but our success had been temporary only as we were bombed off again as soon as it was daylight. On the other hand, the possession of the Máleme landing grounds was vital.[49]

Freyberg planned to attack through the defensive line held east of Máleme by 5th NZ Bde with what remained of the 4th NZ Bde as the CREFORCE reserve while the MNBDO and 10th NZ Bde held their defensive positions. However, events had overtaken

Freyberg as he gave his orders at 5:00 P.M. on 22 May 1941. 10th NZ Bde had conducted a series of spirited counterattacks into the Ayia valley during the day, some personally led by Kippenberger. As with the previous two days, Kippenberger continued to attack and seize ground only to have to withdraw under air attack and mortar fire and surrender ground to Heidrich's 3rd *Fallschirmjäger* Regt that had, during the day, been reinforced and replenished by parachute drops. The blocking of the German attacks from the Ayia Valley severely depleted Kippenberger's composite brigade and drew all available personnel forward to the defensive line deeper in the valley. Consequently, when heavy German attacks along the coastal road and penetrations into 10th NZ Bde area increased, Puttick was faced with the possibility of having 5th NZ Bde, comprising at the time five infantry battalions, defending west of Plantanias cut off from the remainder of his division.

Conducting a counterattack along insecure lines of communication against Máleme that, by last light was estimated to be occupied by five German battalions supported by heavy mortars and artillery,[50] was considered too risky by Hargest and Puttick. Freyberg, no doubt mindful that the operation may result in the destruction of over fifty percent of 2NZEF in a single battle, agreed to the withdrawal of 5th NZ Bde in order to consolidate 2nd NZ Div into one defensive line in the vicinity of Plantanias. Having taken over 2,000 casualties in the Máleme and Canea sectors, Puttick's troops were very low on both ammunition and food, had been fighting for three days without pause, and had lost the majority of the limited armored and artillery support that they started the battle with. Although this decision effectively surrendered Máleme airfield to the enemy and sealed the fate of CREFORCE, it was not a rash decision on Freyberg's behalf to allow the withdrawal. In all likelihood, ordering the continued attack would have destroyed the majority of the New Zealand division. As the commander of 2NZEF, this may have weighed on Freyberg's mind when considering the tactical and operational situation. The loss of the New Zealand division may have been acceptable to his British masters at that stage of the war; however, it would have been catastrophic for New Zealand.

Over the next four days (23-26 May 1941) Ringel continued his relentless buildup through Máleme airfield. On 23 May 1941 3,650 troops airlanded and the remainder of 5th *Gebirgs* Division in the two days that followed to commence attacking east pushing 2nd NZ Div back towards Suda Bay with a series of regimental-sized attacks. More importantly, the *Luftwaffe*, with Máleme outside of effective direct and observed indirect fires range, was able to base aircraft at the airfield. This greatly increased the capability of the *Luftwaffe* to conduct detailed aerial reconnaissance over the entire island and provide intimate support to the attacks on not only Canea, but to the regiments operating in Retimo and Heráklion. Richthofen's VIII *Fliegerkorps* had been ordered to transfer its aircraft from supporting the Crete battle to bases in Poland in order to prepare for Operation Barbarossa from 27 May 1941. Ringel made the most of the air support while he had it, directing relentless attacks and carpet-bombing against Canea to demoralize both the military and civilian population, and trap the defenders in the Canea/Suda Bay pocket.[51]

Freyberg, as he had throughout the first three days, continued to press Wavell for additional support for the defense of Crete. On 22 May 1941 prior to the counterattack, he had requested the Máleme airfield be attacked and the surface damaged to prevent further landings.[52] The requested attack never materialized, however Wavell did send whatever meager assistance was available to him. This later included air attacks (albeit in very limited numbers and with very little effect), and reinforcement by the 'LAYFORCE Commando' commanded by Colonel R. E. Laycock consisting 800 men into the south of Crete and the Argyle and Sutherland Highlanders that reinforced Herákion.[53] Freyberg intended for this battalion, along with Chappel's force, to advance west if possible by road to link up with the Campbell and relieve the pressure on Suda.[54] Freyberg, however, was frustrated by the apparent lack of understanding from his superior commanders about the severity of the situation on Crete:

> I want you to get the true picture so that our difficulties can be appreciated. They have continued to land troop-carriers, not only on the airfield under our shellfire but also on the beaches and a strip to the west, in the most methodical way. In all, fifty-nine landed between 1 P.M. and 4 P.M. today. . . . It was my intention to attack the airfield again tonight but the threat to my rear has forced my hand. I have decided to readjust the present insecure position and make ready for secure defense. The serious situation is that Máleme becomes an operational airfield within 20,000 meters of Suda Bay.[55]

Churchill, confident that armed with the Ultra intelligence Freyberg would defeat the attack, had cabled to Freyberg that "the whole world watches your splendid battle on which great things turn."[56] Even after the Royal Navy had informed Whitehall that they could no longer replenish Freyberg via Suda Bay due to the intensity of air attacks after the defeat of the seaborne flotillas, and must withdraw from the Aegean Sea entirely, there was still an over-optimistic view of the battle at higher levels of command. Freyberg desperately asked for air support through cables to not only Wavell, but also through Fraser to Churchill in an effort to impress on Whitehall the desperate situation that had developed. Fraser cabled Churchill on 24 May 1941:

> I am very anxious about the position in Crete. Although our men are fighting courageously and desperately, the odds against seem to be accumulating. . . . In the name of the New Zealand Government I would strongly urge that all possible additional support by air and sea be immediately provided, and especially the full air assistance that can be released from all quarters, including the United Kingdom.[57]

Churchill was somewhat put out by Fraser's last sentence which he felt implied that additional air assets were being held back in the United Kingdom and cabled Fraser that "there are ample aircraft in the United Kingdom and we have been sending them as fast as possible by every route and every method."[58] Instead of the requested air support, Freyberg received from Middle East Command advice on how to conduct infantry/armored counterattacks and an officer schooled in such operations was even dispatched to Crete by flying boat. The withdrawal of the Royal Navy from the Aegean meant Freyberg was running woefully short of supplies. This was not limited to solely ammunition for fighting, but also food for his force, both of which were fast running out. On 24 May 1941, Freyberg cabled Wavell:

> As I feel we are on the eve of an attack, I want you to know the full picture of the last four days. The fighting has been very fierce and we can definitely say that the much-vaunted parachutists have been heavily defeated. I feel that you should know that the scale of air attack we have been faced with has been far worse than anything I had visualized. It has been savage. Anything you can do to neutralize the air situation would help us materially.[59]

When it dawned upon Churchill and the Whitehall staff that Crete was likely to be lost, Churchill informed Wavell that "victory in Crete essential at this turning-point in the war. Keep hurling in all aid you can."[60] From being an economy of force effort prior to the battle, Churchill was now seemed to suddenly regard Crete as a "key post in the Mediterranean."[61] However, for Freyberg, and to some extent Wavell, it was a case of too little, too late.

Although the defensive line surrounding Canea held up until 26 May 1941, Freyberg realized the battle was lost, and his priority turned to extracting as much of the force from Crete as possible. Freyberg cabled Wavell that the situation had deteriorated to the point where his force was beyond any offensive action, and casualties within the past twenty-four hours had been heavy. Freyberg was convinced that once Canea and Suda had been taken, it was only a matter of time before Retimo and Heráklion fell.[62] Wavell suggested the force fall back to Retimo and hold the eastern part of the island to which Freyberg's reply on 27 May 1941 again demonstrated how perilous the situation had become:

> It is obvious you do not realise the position here. Retimo is practically foodless and without ammunition, and is cut off in every direction. Because of the absence of gun tractors, all artillery in the sector has been lost. We can survive only if food is landed at Sphakia at once. Although our ration strength is large, our effective strength is very small. Unless given adequate air support there is no possibility of our existing as a fighting force. . . . I urge, therefore, that the only course is to go to Sphakia, which seems to give us some chance of saving some of my force. Retimo is also in difficulties unless moved at once. . . . No troops can stand up to 500-pound bombs and our men have been blown out of the ground. What we require is air support.[63]

The collapse of the Canea front sealed the fate of the defense and precipitated the withdrawal south from Canea to Sphakia, forty miles away. Despite desperate brigade counterattacks within the 2nd NZ Div defensive line to deny German penetrations at Galatas on 25 May 1941, command and control was rapidly breaking down. Again, Freyberg was not served well by his subordinate commanders. Freyberg was determined there would be no general retreat and that units would fight through a series of successive organized defensive lines. Both Weston and Puttick were ordered by Freyberg to establish a joint defensive line at Suda under the command of Weston. Some authors feel that Freyberg chose Weston to command the force as he was not satisfied with Puttick's performance in the preceding days. 5th NZ Bde holding part of the line was to be relieved later in the night by the reconstituted 4th NZ Bde and the CREFORCE reserve (consisting 1st Welch and remaining elements of the 1st Rangers, Northumberland Hussars and Royal Perivolians).

The purpose of the defensive line was to allow supplies and reinforcements to disembark at Suda Bay with which to conduct a coordinated defense and withdrawal. This was Freyberg's direction to both Weston and Puttick. A lack of coordination between Weston, Puttick, Vasey (now operating under Weston) and Hargest, compounded by almost non-existent communications, confused the situation. The brigade commanders fighting their individual battles against the fresh 5th *Gebirgs* Div, urged both Puttick and Weston to allow them to withdraw. Weston went to Freyberg's advance headquarters again seeking permission to withdrawal, and was told he must not abandon the defensive line. In a confusing period that immediately followed this discussion on 27 May 1941, Weston failed to inform Puttick by radio, runner or personally, or any of the subordinate units of Freyberg's insistence the line be held, *and* that the force reserve was moving to relieve the forward units. Puttick made the decision to allow the brigades to retire from the line as they saw necessary and commence the withdrawal. In countermanding Freyberg's order to retain the defensive line, Puttick essentially reduced the ability of Freyberg to conduct a coordinated withdrawal. Freyberg, Weston and Puttick spent the remainder of the operation trying to establish control, often without communications between units, of the brigades who were fighting as individual units to the south and evacuation.[64] Despite a series of spirited battles around and south of Canea that including 19th Aust Bde and 5th NZ Bde (under Hargest who at this stage demonstrated more effective leadership than previously) conducting a bayonet charge directly into the 141st *Gebirgsjäger* Regt and LAYFORCE delaying the enemy in the Suda area, the battle was all but lost.

As units from Canea and Suda began withdrawing, Freyberg also attempted to ensure the garrisons at Retimo and Heráklion were effectively supported in their evacuation. On 27 May 1941, he tried to get a message to Campbell to withdraw south toward Sphakia, however efforts on the radio and messengers carried by both boat and air failed. Freyberg had secured enough Royal Navy shipping to evacuate Campbell's force from Retimo on the night of 31 May 1941, but was unable to inform them of the evacuation plan. A failed aerial resupply and counterattack through the German lines towards Suda Bay ended any chance of the forces at Retimo linking up with the remainder of CREFORCE. Campbell fought on at Retimo until 29 May 1941 unaware of the evacuation plan, and when faced with Ringel's forces advancing east supported by artillery, air, and armor landed at Kisamos Kastelli two days previously, was forced to surrender.[65]

Wavell had confirmed the order to evacuate Crete on 27 May 1941, and from 28 May 1941, Cunningham commenced the uplift of CREFORCE from Sphakia and Heráklion. Informed of the evacuation on 28 May 1941 by Freyberg, Chappel had commenced reducing his perimeter at Heráklion in preparation for evacuation by the Royal Navy, under growing pressure from the *Luftwaffe* and reinforcements landed in preparation for further attacks. Three cruisers and six destroyers entered Heráklion harbor on the night of 28 May 1941 and successfully evacuated 4,000 of the 4,200 defenders. Unfortunately, insufficient space precluded evacuation of the wounded and Greek troops.[66] Having successfully defended Heráklion with relatively light casualties, Chappel's force suffered a cruel blow when the *Luftwaffe* attacked the convoy as it withdrew to Alexandria and the 14th (UK) Bde suffered over twenty percent casualties.[67]

Freyberg and Cunningham's evacuation plan of the remainder of CREFORCE planned for 6,000 troops to be evacuated from Sphakia on 29 May 1941, 3000 the following night, and a further 3,000 on 31 May 1941.[68] Freyberg had handed over the rear guard defense to Weston by 28 May 1941, and thereafter coordinated the evacuation from Sphakia until the night of the 30 May 1941, at which time he was personally ordered off Crete by Wavell after refusing to leave the day before. Weston, through the defense of 5th NZ Bde, 19th Aust Bde and LAYFORCE succeeded in delaying the pursuing 5th *Gebirgs* Div to allow the evacuation to occur without serious interference of the embarkation site at Sphakia.

Freyberg earlier predicted only twenty-five percent of the force would be able to be withdrawn, however, "some 17,500 British and Dominion troops were evacuated from Crete to Egypt, of which 13,000 (including 1,500 walking wounded) left from Sphakia. . . . Some 1,751 men had been killed and 12, 254 were made prisoner of war, of whom 700 were stretcher cases."[69] Although the number of British troops taken prisoner of war was high, Freyberg succeeded in withdrawing over sixty percent of the force, the majority of which were the fighting elements of the British, New Zealand and Australian troops that were evacuated as complete units. While on the ground the evacuation may have appeared disorganized, the retention of unit integrity was essential as units were able to be later reconstituted in Africa, before being committed into battle again as battalions, brigades and in the case of 2nd NZ Div, a division. Both Freyberg and Weston had requested the Royal Navy return to Crete on the night of 1 June 1941 and possibly 2 June 1941 to evacuate the remaining troops. Cunningham, however, feared further losses of his already depleted fleet at the hands of the *Luftwaffe* and the Italian Navy, and convinced Whitehall the cost would be too high. Weston departed from Crete on 31 May 1941, and Lieutenant-Colonel Young of LAYFORCE surrendered the remaining British forces to the Germans. The Battle of Crete was over.

---

[1] Callum MacDonald, *The Lost Battle: Crete 1941* (New York: The Free Press, 1993) 79; and Hanson W. Baldwin, *The Crucial Years 1939-1941* (New York: Harper and Row Publishers, 1976), 283-286.

[2] MacDonald, 169.

[3] Paul Freyberg, *Bernard Freyberg VC: Soldier of Two Nations* (Kent, United Kingdom: Hodder and Stoughton, 1991), 305.

[4] Laurie Barber and John Tonkin-Covell, *Freyberg: Churchill's Salamander* (London, United Kingdom: Century Hutchinson Ltd., 1990), 47.

[5] Freyberg, 306.

[6] Geoffrey Cox, *A tale of Two Battles: A Personal Memoir of Crete and the Western Desert 1941* (London: William Kimber & Co. Ltd., 1987), 75.

[7] MacDonald, 188-189.

[8] Barber and Tonkin-Covell, 49.

[9] MacDonald, 199; and Daniel M. Davin, *Official History of New Zealand in the Second World War, 1939-45, Crete* (Wellington, New Zealand: War History Branch, Department of Internal Affairs, 1953), 123-124.

[10] Jim H. Henderson, *Official History of New Zealand in the Second World War, 22 Battalion* (Wellington, New Zealand: War History Branch Department of Internal Affairs, 1949), 70.

[11] Davin, 99-120; and Henderson, 43-45.

[12] Davin, 130-135.

[13] MacDonald, 201; and Henderson, 70-73.

[14]Cox, 78.

[15]Ian Stewart, *The Struggle for Crete: 20 May-1 June 1941, A Story of Lost Opportunity* (London, United Kingdom: Oxford University Press, 1966), 180.

[16]Howard Karl Kippenberger, *Infantry Brigadier* (London, United Kingdom: Oxford University Press, 1949), 53-57.

[17]Davin, 162; and Stewart, 194.

[18]Ibid., 166-167.

[19]Ibid., 168.

[20]Ibid., 169.

[21]Davin 177; and MacDonald 190-191.

[22]Davin 177. and MacDonald 190-191.

[23]Stewart, 201.

[24]MacDonald, 194.

[25]War History Branch New Zealand. *Official History of New Zealand in the Second World War, 1939-45 Documents Relating to New Zealand's Participation in the Second World War 1939-45: Volume I* (Wellington, New Zealand: War History Branch Department of Internal Affairs, 1949), 408.

[26]Stewart, 254.

[27]Freyberg, 301.

[28]Davin, 185-186.

[29]Ibid., 195.

[30]Antony Beevor, *Crete: The Battle and the Resistance* (London, United Kingdom: John Murray Ltd., 1991), 157.

[31]Ibid., 157-158.

[32]Davin, 195.

[33]Ibid., 196.

[34]Davin, 197; and Freyberg 304.

[35] Davin, 198.

[36] Ibid., 198.

[37] Ibid., 208-209.

[38] Beevor, 168.

[39] Davin, 213-214.

[40] Ibid., 215-224.

[41] Freyberg, 303.

[42] Davin, 229-230.

[43] Freyberg, 304.

[44] Ibid., 304.

[45] Freyberg, 302.

[46] Beevor, 180-181.

[47] MacDonald, 225.

[48] Ibid., 210.

[49] Davin, 238.

[50] Ibid., 240.

[51] MacDonald, 255.

[52] War History Branch New Zealand, 413.

[53] Ibid., 415, 417.

[54] Stewart, 364.

[55] Ibid., 417.

[56] Freyberg, 307.

[57] War History Branch New Zealand, 421.

[58] Ibid., 422.

[59] Ibid., 423.

[60] Winston S. Churchill, *The Second World War, Volume 3, The Grand Alliance* (Boston: Houghton Mifflin Company, 1950), 295.

[61] Davin, 272.

[62] War History Branch New Zealand, 428.

[63] Ibid., 429.

[64] Davin, 340-375; and Stewart, 408-420.

[65] MacDonald, 280; and Davin, 387, 390.

[66] Davin, 413.

[67] MacDonald, 285.

[68] Davin, 413.

[69] Freyberg, 312.

CHAPTER 6

AFTERMATH AND CONCLUSION

The outcome of the operational and tactical level battles on, around and above Crete point to a decisive victory for Germany which at the time, was what it was heralded as by the German propaganda machine. However, the defeat of the British ground forces commanded by Freyberg, and to some extent Cunningham's naval forces that were severely attrited, masked the positive strategic outcomes from the battle. Greater coordination in joint operational planning resulted from the hard lessons learnt by not only Middle East Command, but at all levels of the British command chain. The value of airborne operations was not lost on the British and American armies, who accelerated their own airborne programs based upon the observed tactics, techniques and procedures (good as well as bad) from the battle. Integration of antiaircraft, coastal artillery and ground forces including field artillery and armor into coordinated tactical-level defenses commanded by separate services improved in other locations susceptible to airborne envelopment. Hitler, Göring and the *Luftwaffe* learnt different lessons however.

Student, after Crete, retained his belief that the airborne assault was a viable operational concept. He reasoned that he had achieved an operational-level victory without naval support or linking up and being relieved by a ground force, and was confident that the XI *Fliegerkorps* would have further airborne missions. Hitler, however, was appalled by the high number of losses on Crete of both in personnel and aircraft, the single battle costing more lives than the remainder of the Balkans campaign in its entirety, and over 350 aircraft.[1] Hitler informed Student "that we shall never do another airborne operation. Crete proved that the days of the parachute troops are over. The parachute arm is one that relies entirely on surprise. In the meantime, the surprise factor has exhausted itself."[2]

The success of the German attack was attributed in *Airborne Operations: A German Appraisal* to the purely defensive measures adopted by the defenders and failure to immediately counterattack the landings, the committal of the 5th *Gebirgs* Div *en masse* into the most favorable lodgment, and the systematic attack of these forces immediately after landing. Earlier and more detailed reconnaissance of landing zones was seen as the greatest failing of the operation along with the ability of the British Navy to control the sea surrounding the island.[3] The *Luftwaffe* conducted two further airborne operations after Crete, neither above battalion strength, into Leros in 1943 and the Ardennes in 1944. Leros was a supporting effort to a seaborne operation and the Ardennes operation, a desperate measure, failed due to poor weather and Allied air superiority. The greatest strategic effect of the battle was that OKW abandoned plans to seize the island of Malta by airborne forces (based and supported from Italy) after Crete. Had Student managed to capture Crete with relatively low casualties, it is likely Hitler would have launched an airborne-centric mission soon after Crete to seize this dominant strategic British outpost and therefore dominate the Mediterranean. That Hitler and OKW did not further use or develop Crete after the battle for any offensive purpose, strengthens the conclusion that seizing the island was solely a defensive measure to deny it as an air and naval base to the British, therefore securing the flank for Operation Barbarossa.

The aftermath of the battle of Crete and Freyberg's culpability is best examined from three perspectives. Firstly, in view of the actions and opinions expressed by Freyberg's subordinates immediately after the battle; secondly, the official inquiries at the instigation of Churchill and Fraser; and lastly, Freyberg's own comments in official summaries and responses to inquiries post-battle and in his recollections and opinions recorded after the war. As with any battle, the analysis of an operation differs over time, when additional sources become available and are considered. This most definitely occurred with the aftermath of the Battle of Crete. Official inquiries that occurred immediately after the battle were without the benefit of later writings that had access to not only Ultra, but also German officers involved in Operation Merkur and their documents. Individual opinions, and the emotion of having just fought a losing battle, were also all apparent in the immediate analysis of why the Battle of Crete was lost by the British forces.

The post-battle inquiries directed by Churchill and Fraser were tainted against Freyberg by the comments and conduct of two New Zealand senior officers, Inglis and Hargest. Inglis, who flew to London directly after the battle, had an audience with Churchill on 13 June 1941,[4] the first officer involved in the battle to do so. At the meeting, he expressed his own views on the battle and the reasons why it was lost. Inglis was a brigade commander with only a limited view of the operational battlefield, however sought to apportion blame for tactical and operational failures up the command chain to Freyberg and Wavell's level. This attitude was mirrored by the actions of Hargest in Cairo. Hargest met Fraser (before Freyberg had the opportunity to) and was highly critical of Freyberg's handling of both the withdrawal from Greece and the defense of Crete.[5] As with Inglis, Hargest failed to mention any of the shortcomings in his own performance on Crete to Fraser. The comments of both these officers, in private to Churchill and Fraser, and later in public, would taint Freyberg's relationship with both prime ministers but also with the New Zealand public. For Freyberg, the disloyalty demonstrated by these two senior officers, firstly for stepping outside the chain of command, and for their comments, shaped their future relationships. This included Freyberg choosing other senior New Zealand officers to lead 2nd NZ Div in his absence over the more experienced and senior Inglis.

Churchill directed on 14 June 1941 an official Court of Inquiry be conducted by the Chiefs of Staff Committee into the conduct of the battle. His opinion, shaped by Inglis, of Freyberg's handling of the battle was not favorable prior to the inquiry:

> I am far from reassured about the tactical conduct of the defense by General Freyberg. . . . There appears to have been no counter attack of any kind in the western sector, until more than thirty-six hours after the airborne descents had begun. There was no attempt to form a mobile reserve with the best troops, be it only a couple of battalions. There is no attempt to obstruct the Máleme airfield, although General Freyberg knew that he would have no Air in the battle. The whole seems to have been a static defense of positions, instead of the rapid extirpation at all costs of the airborne landing party. It was lucky, however, that the troops got away when they did.[6]

The Court of Inquiry was a tri-service committee led by Brigadier-General A. G. Salisbury-Jones, and was completed by July 1941. The report concluded:

> The major lesson of this campaign was that to defend with a relatively small force an island as large as Crete, lying under permanent domination of enemy fighter aircraft and out of range of our own, was impossible.
> (a) Up to the last neither the Chiefs of Staff nor the C-in-C, ME gave due weight to the vulnerability of the Navy and Merchant Ships.
> (b) The Royal Air Force cannot claim to have shown greater foresight or energy than the Army.
> (c) The planning of operations such as the defense of Crete demands exceptional foresight and the most intimate cooperation between the Services if due weight is to be given to the many factors involved.
> (d) The Committee are of the opinion that until the eleventh hour no Service gave due weight to the preponderating factor affecting this problem, which was the overwhelming superiority of the German Air Force.[7]

Whilst this report favorably recognized the spirited resistance conducted by Freyberg and the troops, and the heavy losses inflicted on the enemy, it was scathing in the evaluation of Middle East Command in the preparation of the defense of the island, and the support provided to Freyberg once the battle commenced.[8] However, the report was intercepted by Middle East Command before it could be presented to Whitehall and was subsequently suppressed by Wavell. This occurred for two reasons according to Freyberg. Firstly, because of the level of criticism directed at Middle East Command and HQ RAF Middle East; and secondly, because the report breeched security in reference to Ultra. A subsequent "watered down" report was raised by Middle East Command and became the official response until the original was released to public view in 1972.[9] Regardless of the report submitted, Churchill had lost faith in Wavell by the conclusion of the battle, and he was replaced by General Sir Claude Auchinleck as GOC Middle East.

Fraser also sought to establish, on behalf of the New Zealand government, the reasons for the loss of Crete, and to determine if Freyberg should be replaced as the Commander 2NZEF and 2nd NZ Div. He submitted a detailed questionnaire to Churchill about the Balkans operation (including both Greece and Crete) that questioned the support that Freyberg received to conduct the operation. The Chiefs of Staff concluded that the operational circumstances could not have been prevented the battle occurring, and despite the failings of Middle East Command, as much support to Freyberg as possible, was provided.[10] Fraser, in his discussions with Churchill, Wavell and senior commanders other than Hargest and Inglis, was convinced that Freyberg should be retained as the senior New Zealand commander. This was a sound decision for two reasons. Firstly, other than Kippenberger (who was too junior), no other senior New Zealand commander had demonstrated that they could have performed better than Freyberg did; and secondly, in hindsight, Freyberg's performance throughout the remainder of the war in training and leading 2NZEF was exemplary. After "clearing the air" in Cairo, Freyberg and Fraser retained a "harmonious and satisfactory association . . . for the rest of the war."[11]

Freyberg's official report of the battle was sent on 12 September 1941 to the New Zealand Minister of Defense, and summarized the operations in both Greece and Crete. This report detailed the conduct of the subordinate units, and points to the ordering of 6th NZ Bde and 6th Field Regiment (artillery) to Egypt during the withdrawal from Greece, the lack of supplies, and the overwhelming enemy air superiority as factors that influenced the outcome of the battle.[12] Freyberg's personal views, especially with respect to the handling of Ultra, the security limitations he felt were placed upon him, and the capability and conduct of his subordinate commanders were expressed only after the war. Paul Freyberg's biography of his father published in 1991; and Freyberg's personal papers, which he made available for the writing of the *Official History of New Zealand in the Second World War* record his thoughts better on the battle. In these, Freyberg expands on his earlier conclusions to include the unrelenting method in which the German forces reinforced the lodgment at Máleme regardless of personnel or aircraft casualties, and the difficulty in commanding such a fluid battle with intermittent and unreliable communications, under constant air attack.

In determining the overall culpability of Freyberg for the lost battle of Crete, this thesis has analyzed not only Freyberg's own actions and decisions but also those that were outside of his control. To blame Freyberg, owing to him being the senior commander on the ground, is identifying an easy scapegoat as many did after the battle, both in military and civilian circles. Freyberg always accepted responsibility for the defeat as a good commander should, but most military professionals and historians have also identified other factors that were beyond his control contributed to the fall of Crete.

Freyberg assumed command of CREFORCE having just fought his division against the might of the German *Blitzkrieg* through the length of Greece in a battle that was fought for political expediency rather than for definitive political and military objectives. The Battle of Crete took place within the greater overall strategic environment that saw Britain and her allies reeling from defeat to defeat in the face of the awesome power of the German military machine. Accordingly, resources allocated from the strategic level to Freyberg, as the operational commander were insufficient to complete the task assigned him, especially in communications, armor and artillery. Of even greater impact was the decisive absence of the RAF during the operation. Even a modicum of air parity would likely have been the difference in the outcome of the battle. Stewart in *The Struggle for Crete: A Story of Lost Opportunity, 20 May–1 June 1941* accurately sums up the air situation during the Battle of Crete:

> Only from the men who fought in Crete can the truth be known. And for them the matter has always been plain. With them there remains a single vision that surpasses all else – the memory of the absolute domination held by their enemies in the air. . . . In this battle, the defense had neither antiaircraft weapons that might have held the planes at a distance, nor the wireless communications that could have spared the need for exposure, or ordered it better when it became unavoidable.[13]

The island of Crete itself did not lend itself to defense against an airborne invasion. Little preparation by the existing garrison before Freyberg arrived was testimony to the lack of priority Middle East Command assigned it. The attempt to fortify the island and defend it once the Battle for Greece had been decided compounded this strategic error and placed Freyberg at a disadvantage from the start. While Cunningham fought a determined and courageous naval operation around Crete to supply, defend, and then evacuate CREFORCE, this was in itself a forlorn hope against the *Luftwaffe* without Allied air cover.

In Student, Freyberg faced a competent and determined opponent, who had developed and tested a new form of warfare in *vertical envelopment*. Buoyed by the success of the 7th *Flieger* Div and the 22nd *Luftlande* Div operations in Holland, and the rapid defeat of W Force in Greece, Crete provided an ideal opportunity for Student to demonstrate the operational-level capability of the *Luftwaffe* in an air-ground operation. Despite the intelligence failings and difficulties in coordination of initial airborne and fighter aircraft, Student, and later Ringel's relentless drive to reinforce the lodgment, regardless of casualties, determined the outcome of the battle from the German perspective. Although many German soldiers were killed on Crete, the fighting spirit and leadership of the airborne and mountain troops should not be understated or discounted in their securing victory. These were the most professional soldiers of the German Air Force and Army.

The overwhelming dominance of the *Luftwaffe* was the determining factor in the Battle of Crete. The physical numerical superiority in fighters and bombers totally overwhelmed whatever RAF aircraft were in the operational area, driving them out of range to support effectively Freyberg. The number of Royal Navy ships the *Luftwaffe* sunk during the battle essentially isolated Crete by day and, in the absence of the RAF, denied Freyberg naval gunfire support that might have overcome his own indirect fire deficiencies.

The mission given to Freyberg by Wavell was to "to deny Crete to the enemy."[14] Ultra intelligence gave Freyberg the most detailed understanding of the enemy's plan by any commander to that stage of the war. This intelligence did not however determine the weighting of effort in each of the three sectors that the *Luftwaffe* had determined as drop zones, nor did it accurately weight the seaborne invasion. Freyberg did make some faulty assumptions in relation to the intelligence, but none that would not have seemed feasible at the time. Freyberg should be faulted for his defensive disposition at Máleme and failure to defend the Tavronitis River area with troops on the ground, however, as events played out this fault was only magnified by the failure of subordinate units to counterattack into this area to defeat the enemy. Freyberg's handling of Ultra intelligence, and some of the decisions he made in relation to it (such as not moving forces to the Tavronitis River), may have over-emphasized the security restrictions and his responsibility to safeguard the source. However, he could not defend against all possibilities. Both Bennett and Keegan were correct in concluding that "both force as well as foreknowledge is needed to win battles."[15]

Freyberg's method of defense given his resources and the terrain was correct. Each sector possessed the resources to defend against the airborne attack, and to counterattack to defeat enemy lodgments. This was demonstrated by Chappel, Campbell and Kippenberger effectively during the first two days. The failure of Hargest, Puttick and to some extent Inglis to comply with this direction (and CREFORCE Operation Order No. 10) resulted in defeat for CREFORCE. Compliance, immediately, with

Freyberg's direction on the night of 20 May 1941 by 2nd NZ Div, and as late as 22 May 1941, would have likely changed the course of the battle. If the 7th *Flieger* Div had been defeated in the first day, it is unlikely that Student, Göring or Hitler would have called off the attack on Crete. A diversion of resources from Operation Barbarossa is also unlikely, but an Allied operational victory may have been secured, and a retirement out of contact from the island conducted before the Germans attacked again.

Throughout the conduct of the battle, Freyberg was frustrated by the lack of communications with which to command CREFORCE. This capability, second probably only to air support, contributed to the defeat of the British forces, and was felt at all levels of command. Had effective communications existed, Andrew probably would never have withdrawn back from Hill 107 on the first night, the counterattack by 20th Bn and 28th (Maori) Bn would have been coordinated better, and the collapse of the defensive line at Canea could have been prevented. Out of touch with superior and subordinate headquarters, commanders were forced to either make decisions on their own understanding of the battle, or worse, as occurred numerous times, make no decision at all. As Lewin concluded in *Ultra Goes To War,* "it has been said that a hundred radios would have saved Crete."[16]

The Battle of Crete was an intense operation that pitted German air power and crack airborne troops against British naval power and spirited defenders. Freyberg was a consummate professional Army officer who immediately accepted, as the CREFORCE commander, and regardless of other circumstances, responsibility for the defeat. He never sought to apportion blame on any subordinate officer, on any of the services, or his superior officers. Freyberg did make some errors prior to and during the battle, but they do not constitute the sole source for the defeat of CREFORCE. Given the operational and strategic circumstances that he and his troops were placed in, the strength and competence of his enemy, and the failure of some of his subordinates to prosecute his operational plan, Freyberg cannot be held culpable for the loss of Crete.

---

[1] Antony Beevor, *Crete: The Battle and the Resistance* (London, United Kingdom: John Murray Ltd., 1991), 230.

[2] A. H. Farrar-Hockley, *Student* (New York: Ballantine Books Inc., 1973), 100-101.

[3] Department of the Army, Pamphlet, No. 20-232, *Airborne Operations: A German Appraisal* (Washington, DC: Centre of Military History, October 1951), 19-20.

[4] Beevor, 228.

[5] Laurie Barber and John Tonkin-Covell, *Freyberg: Churchill's Salamander* (London, United Kingdom: Century Hutchinson Ltd., 1990), 110-111.

[6] Ibid., 113.

[7] Paul Freyberg, *Bernard Freyberg VC: Soldier of Two Nations* (Kent, United Kingdom: Hodder and Stoughton, 1991), 315.

[8] Ibid., 315.

[9] Ibid., 316-319.

[10] W. G. McClymont, *Official History of New Zealand in the Second World War, 1939-45, To Greece* (Wellington, New Zealand: War History Branch Department of Internal Affairs, 1959), 491-514.

[11] Freyberg, 335.

[12] War History Branch New Zealand. *Official History of New Zealand in the Second World War, 1939-45 Documents Relating to New Zealand's Participation in the Second World War 1939-45: Volume II* (Wellington, New Zealand: War History Branch Department of Internal Affairs, 1949), 16-21.

[13] Ian Stewart, *The Struggle for Crete: 20 May-1 June 1941, A Story of Lost Opportunity* (London, United Kingdom: Oxford University Press, 1966), 323-324.

[14] Freyberg, 267.

¹⁵John Keegan, *Intelligence in War* (New York: Vintage Books, 2002), 179.

¹⁶Ronald Lewin, *Ultra Goes To War* (New York: McGraw-Hill Book Company, 1978), 156.

APPENDIX A

MAP OF THE EASTERN MEDITERRANEAN

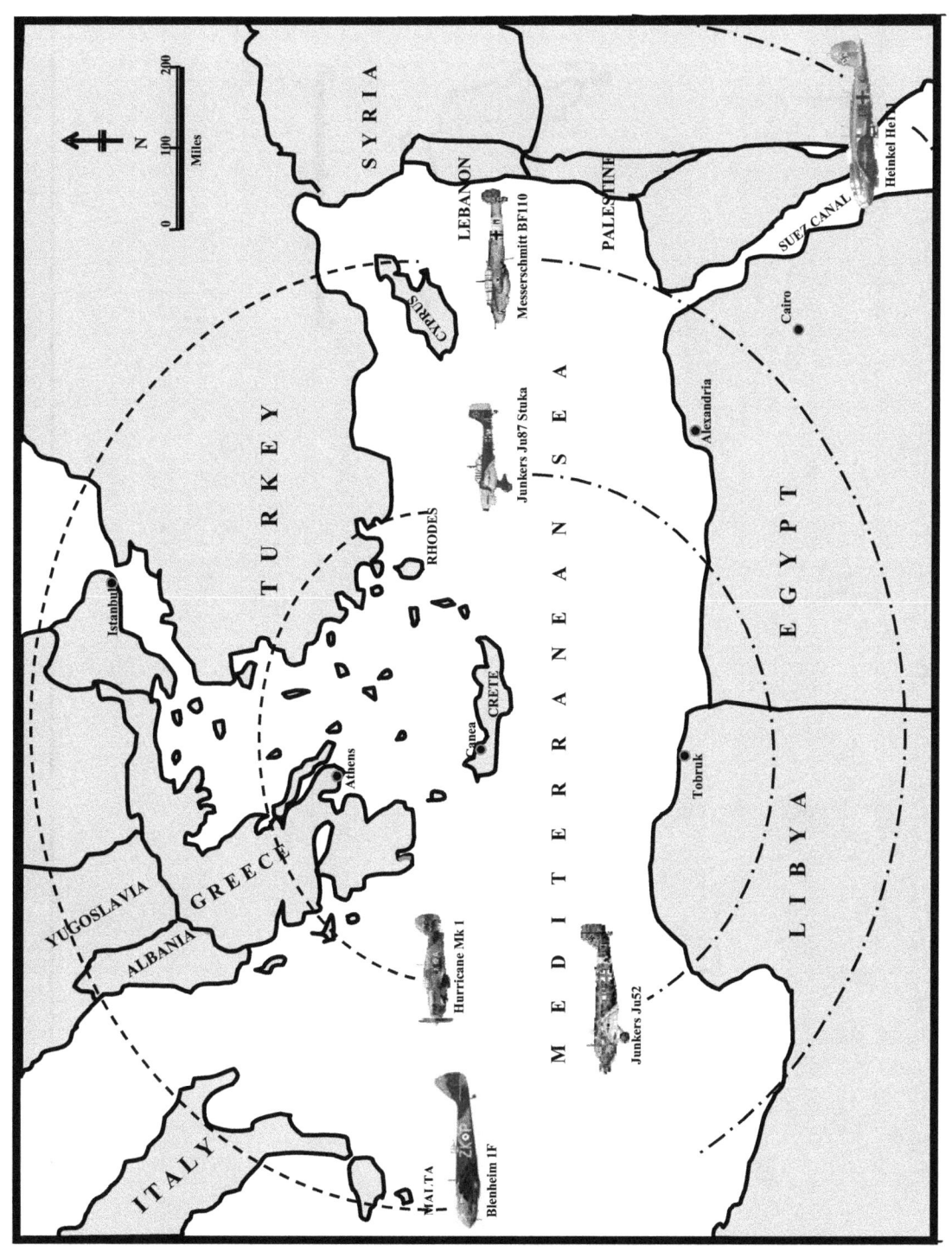

APPENDIX B

MAP OF CRETE

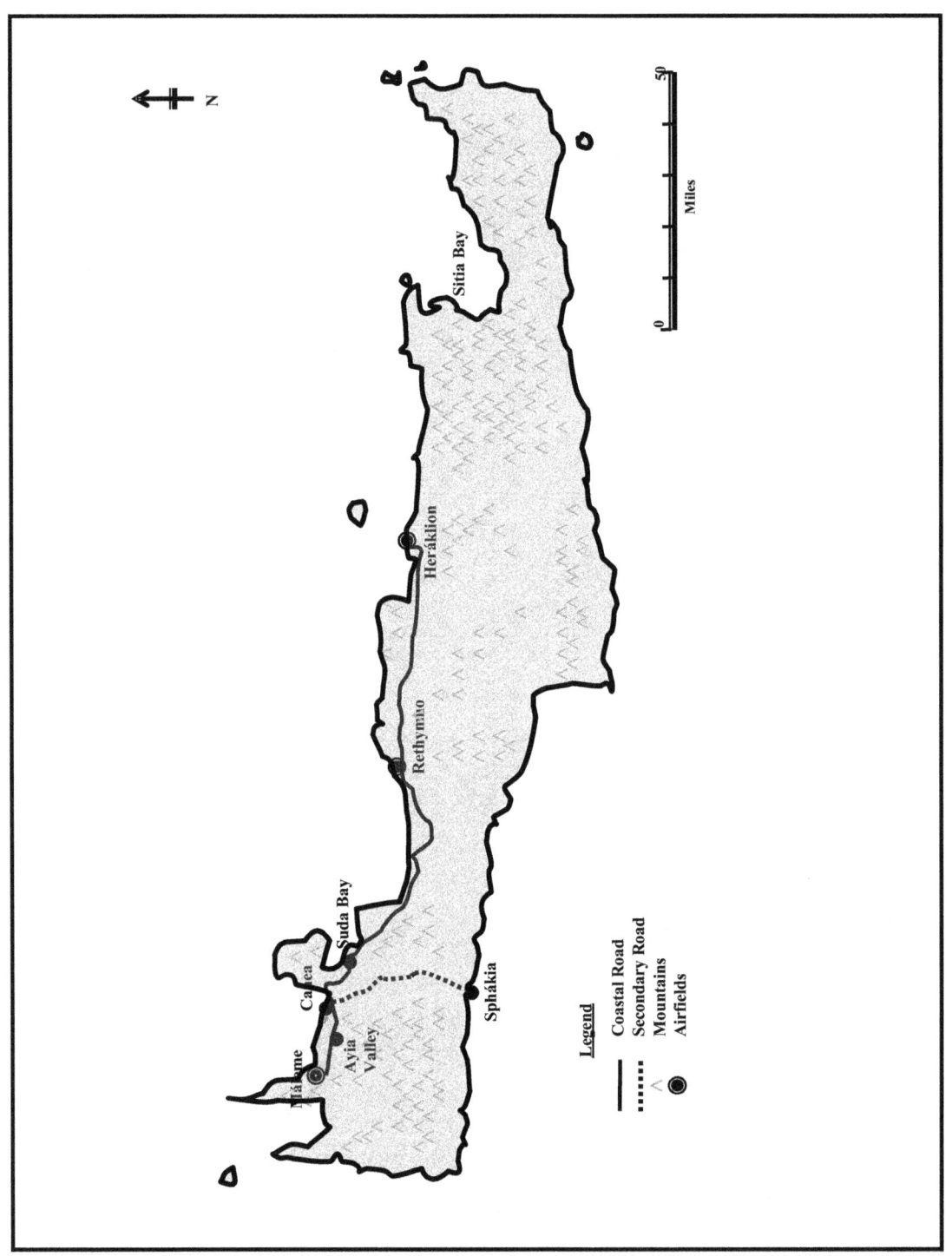

APPENDIX C

GERMAN ORDER OF BATTLE (OPERATION MERKUR)

Luftwaffe	*Generalfeldmarschal* Göring
	Generaloberst Jeschonnek (Chief of Staff)
IV *Luftflotte*	*Generaloberst* Löhr
VIII *Fliegerkorps*	*General der Flieger* Freiherr von Richthofen

120 Dornier 17s based at Tatoi
40 Heinkel 111s based at Eleusis
80 Junkers 88s based at Eleusis
150 Junkers 87b Stukas based at Mycenae, Molaöi and Skarpanto
90 Messerschmitt 110s based at Argos
90 Messerschmitt 109s based at Molaöi

XI *Fliegerkorps*   *Generaloberst* Student

Three transport groups under command (approximately 500 Junkers 52s)
Glider Wing (approximately 70 DFS 230 gliders)
Sqn of Fieseler Storch reconnaissance aircraft

HQ *Luftlande Sturmregiment*   *Generalmajor* Meindl
I Bn
II Bn
III Bn
IV Bn

7th *Flieger* **Div**   *Generalmajor* Süssmann

Parachute Engineer Bn

HQ 1st *Fallschirmjäger* Regt   *Oberst* Bräuer
I Bn
II Bn
III Bn

HQ 2nd *Fallschirmjäger* Regt   *Oberst* Strum
I Bn
II Bn
III Bn

HQ 3rd *Fallschirmjäger* Regt   *Oberst* Heidrich
I Bn
II Bn
III Bn

5th *Gebirg* Div   *Generalmajor* Ringel

95th *Gebirgsjäger* Regt (Div troops)
Mountain Artillery Bn
Pioneer Bn
Reconnaissance Bn

85th *Gebirgsjäger* Regt   *Oberst* Krakaus
I Bn
II Bn
III Bn

100th *Gebirgsjäger* Regt   *Oberst* Utz
I Bn
II Bn
III Bn

141st *Gebirgsjäger* Regt (6th *Gebirg* Div)   *Oberst* Jais
I Bn
II Bn
III Bn

Strength

Landed by parachute and glider:	
Máleme	1,860
Ayia Valley and Canea	2,460
Retimo	1,380
Heráklion	2,360
Landed by Troop-Carrier:	
Máleme	13,980
Total by Air (by D+2)	22,040
Seaborne Force:	Approx 7,000
Total Forces:	Approx 29,040

Source: Antony Beevor, *Crete: The Battle and the Resistance* (London, United Kingdom: John Murray Ltd., 1991), 347-348.

APPENDIX D

OPERATION MERKUR PLAN

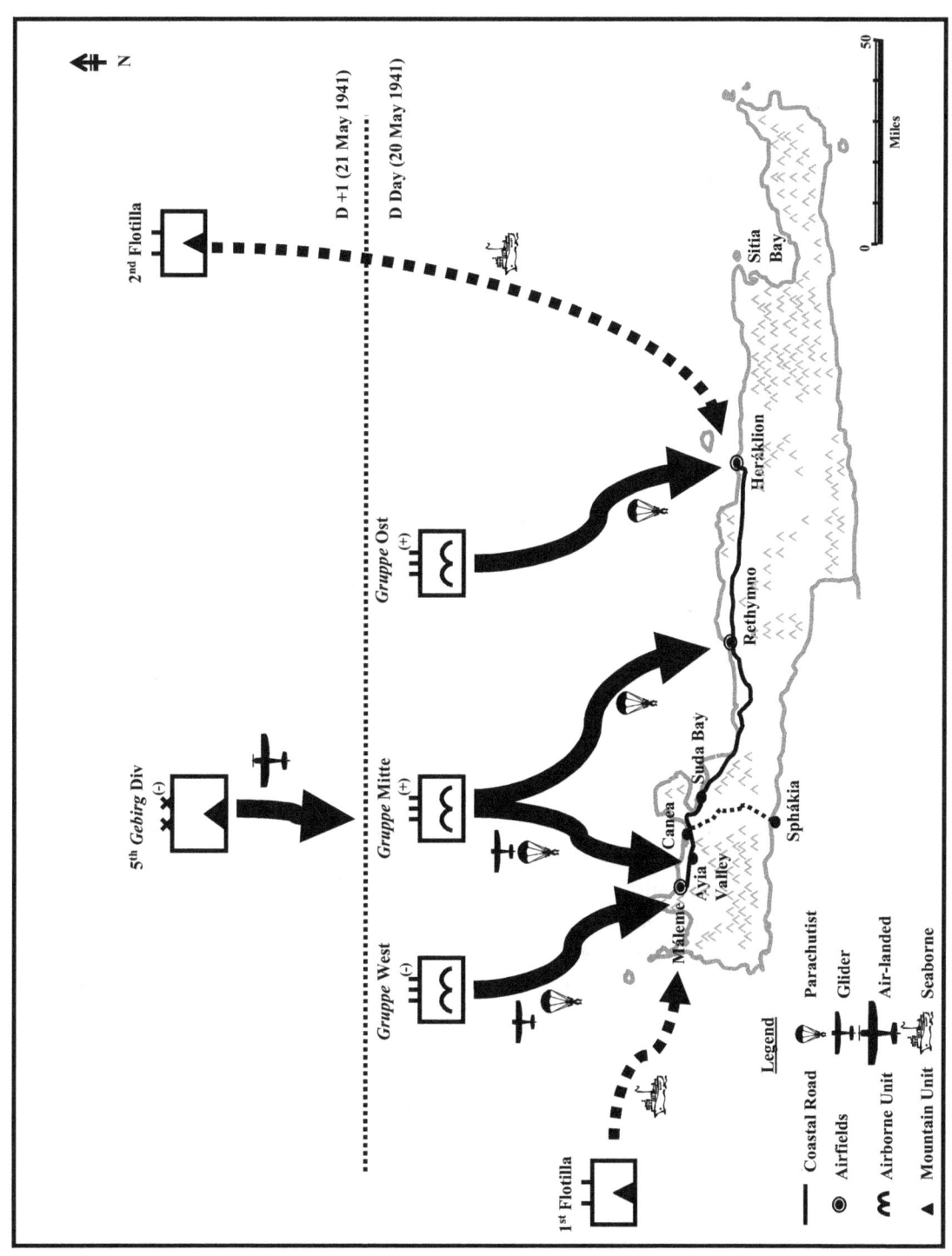

APPENDIX E

ULTRA SIGNALS

Listed below are relevant messages that were received in Crete prior to the battle commencing on 20 May 1941. Once Freyberg arrived on Crete, and after being briefed on Ultra, the messages were sent to him directly encoded. The message was then decoded by Captain Sandover, read by Freyberg and then burned.

OL 2151   1845 hours   28.4.41
OL messages sent to Cairo only will carry OL three digit numbers in current series. Messages to Cairo and A.O.C. Crete (Group Captain Beamish received Ultra for a few days before Freyberg's arrival) carry OL 2000 and up in current series. Numbers thus show distribution each message.

OL 2155   1615 hours   1.5.41
It is learnt that to enable the GAF (German Air Force) to carry out operations planned for the coming weeks, enemy will not mine Suda Bay nor destroy airfields on Crete. This message cancels OL 2154.

OL 2157   0325 hours   3.5.41
There are indications that air transport units will not be ready for large scale operations before 6th May earliest. Other preparations appear to be complete.

OL 2165   2150 hours   4.5.41
There is evidence that on 4th May staff of 7th Fliegerdivision moved to Salonika, and that it will move to Athens about May 8th.

OL 2167   2340 hours   6.5.41
Preparation of operations against Crete probably complete on 17 May. Sequence of operations from zero day onward will be parachute landing of 7th Fliegerdivision plus corps troops 11th Fliegerkorps to seize Máleme Candia (Heráklion) and Retimo (Retimo). The dive bombers and fighters will move to Máleme and Candia. Next air landing of remainder 11th Fliegerkorps including headquarters and subordinate army units. Then flak units further troops and supplies. Third mountain regiment from 12th Army detailed elements of armoured units motorcyclists antitank units to be detailed by supreme command army and all to be under 11th Fliegerkorps. Admiral South-East will provide protection with Italian torpedo boat (or boats?) flotillas minesweepers and possibly U boats. Sea transport by German and Italian vessels. Operation to be preceded before zero day by sharp attack on RAF military camps and antiaircraft positions.

OL2168   1005 hours   7.5.41
Flak units further troops and supplies mentioned our 2167 are to proceed by sea to Crete. Also three mountain regiments thought more likely than third mountain regiment.

OL2169   1735 hours   7.5.41
Melos to be occupied by Germans on 7th May with a view to preparation airfield.

OL2170   1830 hours   7.5.41
Further to 2167 this series concerning projected attack on Crete. Following is estimated scale of attack and suggested timetable. Suggested timetable. First day or first day minus one – sharp bombing attack on air force and military objectives. First day – parachute landings and arrival of some operational aircraft. On first or second day arrival of air landing troops with equipment including guns, motorcycles and possibly light AFVs (armoured fighting vehicles). Second day – arrival of seaborne forces and supplies after arrival of airlanding detachments. Estimated scale of parachute and air landing attack. Number of troop carrying aircraft at present available in the area is about 450. This could be increased to 600 if required. Subject to operational facilities for the highest number being the scale of a parachute attack on the first day could be 12,000 men in two sorties. Scale of air landing of troops and equipment on second day could be 4,000 men, and four hundred tons of equipment or equivalent, carried by 600 Ju 52s. If an air landing operation took place on the first day parachutists effort would be reduced by about 50%. A preliminary bombing attack would probably be made by long range bombers and twin engined fighters based in Bulgaria Salonika Athens and possibly Rhodes. Maximum effort for a day estimated at 105 long range bomber sorties and 100 twin engined fighter sorties. Aircraft available as occupying air force – 60 Me 109s and 90 Ju 87s. Start from landing ground in Peleponnese. Position of landing grounds not known but Germans are believed to be searching for suitable sites. Athens area is the operational area from which airborne attack will probably start. All above scales of effort are the maximum weight which is believed could be attained. No account has been taken of effect our action or possible lack of operational facilities in the Athens area for the maximum number of aircraft available. Foregoing from director of intelligence.

OL 2/284   1900 hours   13.5.41
Twin engined aircraft will probably attack airfields on Crete on May 14th.

OL 2/302   1745 hours   13.5.41
The following summarises intentions against Crete from operations orders issued.
Para 1. The island of Crete will be captured by the 11th Air Corps and the 7th Air Division and the operation will be under the control of the 11th Air Corps.
Para2. All preparations, including the assembly of transport aircraft, fighter aircraft, and dive bomber aircraft, as well as of troops to be carried by both by air and sea transport, will be completed on 17th May.
Para 3. Transport of seaborne troops will be in coordination with admiral south-east, who will ensure the protection of German and Italian transport vessels by Italian light naval forces. These troops will come under the orders of the 11th Air Corps immediately on landing at Crete.
Para 4. A sharp attack by bomber and heavy fighter units to deal with the allied air forces on the ground as well as with their antiaircraft defenses and military camps will precede the operation.

Para 5. The following operations will be carried out from as from day one. The 7th Air Division will make a parachute landing and seize Máleme, Candia, and Retimo. Secondly, dive bombers and fighters (about 100 aircraft of each type) will move by air to Máleme and Candia. Thirdly. Air landing of 11th Air Corps, including air corps headquarters and elements of the Army placed under its command probably including the 22nd Division. Fourthly. Arrival of the seaborne contingent consisting of antiaircraft batteries as well as of more troops and supplies.

Para 6. In addition the 12th Army will allot three Mountain Regiments as instructed. Further elements consisting of motor-cyclists, armoured units, antitank units, antiaircraft units will also be allotted.

Para 7. Depending on the intelligence which is now awaited, also as the result of air reconnaissance, the airfield at Kastelli (Pediados) south east of Candia and the district west and south west of Canea will be specially dealt with, in which case separate instructions will be included in detailed operation orders.

Para 8. Transport aircraft, of which a sufficient number – about 600 – will be allotted for this operation, will be assembled on airfields in the Athens area. The first sortie will probably carry parachute troops only. Further sorties will be concerned with the transport of the air landing contingent, equipment and supplies, and will probably include aircraft towing gliders.

Para 9. With a view to providing fighter protection to the operations, the possibility of establishing a fighter base on Skarpanto will be examined.

Para 10. The Quartermaster General's branch will ensure that adequate fuel supplies for the whole operation are available in the Athens area in good time, and an Italian tanker will be arriving at the Piraeus before 17th May. This tanker will probably also be available to transport fuel supplies to Crete. In assembling supplies and equipment the for invading force it will be borne in mind that it will consist of some 30 to 35,000 men, of which some 12,000 will be the parachute landing contingent, and 10,000 will be transported by sea. The strength of the long range bomber and heavy fighter force which will prepare the invasion by attacking before day one will be of approximately 150 long range bombers and 100 heavy fighters.

Para 11. Orders have been issued that Suda Bay is not to be mined, nor will Cretan airfields be destroyed, so as not to interfere with the operations intended.

Para 12. Plottings prepared from air photographs of Crete on one over ten thousand scale will be issued to units participating in this operation.

OL 5/313   0420 hours   14.5.41

If reconnaissance fails to reveal shipping targets on 14th May Junkers 88 dive bombers gruppe 1 LG1 will attack Suda Bay.

OL 6/314   1015 hours   14.5.41

In future the word Colorado will be used instead of the word Crete in all messages in this series.

OL 8/337   0500 hours   16.5.41

On 16th May attacks by heavy fighters on British aircraft at Heráklion airfield intended also transfer to Scarpanto – airfield probably south point of island – of about 20 Junkers 87 to close Kaso strait.

OL 9/339   0805 hours   16.5.41
Further evidence indicates that day one for operation against Colorado on 17th May but postponement by 48 hours appears likely.

OL 10/431   1410 hours   16.5.41
From further information postponement day one for operation against Colorado confirmed. 19th May seems earliest date.

OL 12/370   0155 hours   19.5.41
On May 19th at 0800 hours GMT conference of officers commanding air force units will take place at Eleusis airfield. Discussions concern operation against Colorado, particular Malemes, Canea Retimo and Iraklion. Sorties by all units in spite of the conference. Single-engined fighters for Malaoi – in strength of about one flight at a time – will repeatedly attack aircraft on Malemes airfield on 19th. Dive bombers on Scarpanto also expected to operate probably on shipping. It seems today Monday may be day minus one.

Source: Antony Beevor, *Crete: The Battle and the Resistance* (London, United Kingdom: John Murray Ltd., 1991), 349-352.

APPENDIX F

CREFORCE OPERATION ORDER

Creforce Operation Instruction No. 10 　　　　　　　　Copy No. 21
　　　　　　　　　　　　　　　　　　　　　　　　　　　　3rd May 1941

APPRECIATION
1. Enemy will attack on CRETE can be expected at any time. It will probably take the following forms:-
   (a) Intensive bombing and M.G. attack on airfields and vicinity.
   (b) Landing by parachutists to clear obstacles and seize airfields.
   (c) Landing by troops in tp carrying aircraft. It is possible, though unlikely that landings may be made at places other than airfields.
2. Seaborne attack must also be expected. This will probably be attempted on beaches close to airfields and/or to SUDA BAY.
3. With the forces at our disposal, it is not possible to oppose the enemy at every place where he might land. The scheme of defense will therefore be based on defending the three airfields, HERÁKLION, RETIMO, and MÁLEME, and the area SUDA BAY, with a centrally placed Force reserve ready to move in any direction.

INTENTION
4. CRETE will be denied to the enemy.
5. *HERÁKLION Sector*
   Comd Brig Chappel
   Tps　 14 Inf Bde less 1 Welch
   　　　 7 Med Regt RA (rifles)
   　　　 2/4 Aust Bn
   　　　 156 Lt AA Bty less two tps
   　　　 One tp and one sec 7 Aust Lt AA Bty (in support)
   　　　 One sec B Bty 15 Coast Regt (in support)
   　　　 Two Greek Bns
6. *RETIMO Sector*
   Comd Brig Vasey
   Tps　 19 Aust Bde HQ
   　　　 2/1 Aust Bn
   　　　 2/7 Aust Bn
   　　　 2/11 Aust Bn
   　　　 1 Aust MG Coy
   　　　 Two Greek Bns

Left boundary all incl: ARMYRO (Gergeoupolis, B 3340) – ASKIFOU, (B 2362)

7. *SUDA BAY Sector*
   Comd Maj-Gen Weston
   Tps　 MNDBO

        1 Welch
        NH
        2/8 Aust Bn (2 rifle companies only)
        151 Hy AA Bty
        234 Hy AA Bty
        129 Lt AA Bty
        7 Aust Lt AA Bty, less two tps and one sec

304 S/L Bty
15 Coast Regt, less one sec Base Sub Area
1 Greek Bn.

8. *MÁLEME Sector*
    Comd Brig Puttick
    Tps   NZ Div
            4 NZ Bde
            5 NZ Bde
            Oakes Force
            Two tps 156 Lt AA Bty (in support)
            One tp 7 Aust Lt AA Bty (in support)

9. *Force Reserve*
1 Welch in SUDA BAY sector and 4 NZ Bde less one bn in Máleme sector are in Force Reserve. They will be administered by respective Sector Comds, but will be concentrated and ready to move on short notice on orders from Force HQ. Comd 1 Welch will be in close touch with Comd 4 NZ Bde.

10. *Policy of Defense*
Sector Comds will organize their sectors so that of the troops allotted to the defense of airfields, one third is disposed on or around the landing ground, and two thirds are kept at such a distance that they will be outside the area which will be attacked in the first instance.

11. Possible landing areas other than airfields will also be protected in similar manner on a smaller scale.

12. In addition, possible sea landing places will be watched, and if resources permit held by troops.

13. It is important that each sector should have a sector reserve.

A.A. DEFENSE

14. Concealment is of paramount importance. All tps whether in reserve or in forward positions must be well dug in. During air attack, both weapons and men must be under cover.

15. Tps in concealed areas will NOT open small arms fire on aircraft unless they have been located and are attacked by aircraft, or the aircraft is about to land.

16. Major General Weston will co-ordinate all A.A. arty on the island.

STATE OF READINESS

17. Attention is directed to CREFORCE Operation Instruction No. 4. Irrespective of the degrees of readiness in force, all tps will "stand to" at dawn and dusk.

R.E. STORES

18. R.E. Stores are allocated as follows:-

Sector	Wire Coils	Pickets Short	Long	Shovels
HERAKLION Sector	1000	1200	1000	75
RETIMO Sector	1000	1500	1000	90
SUDA BAY Sector	700	900	700	60
MÁLEME Sector	2800	3000	2800	200

Sectors will draw direct from R.E. Stores, 42 Street, road SUDA-CANEA, as required.

ADMINISTRATION

19. Issued Separately.

INTERCOMMUNICATION

20. In future, all correspondence, orders, etc., will be addressed to Sector Comds and NOT units of formations.

Source: Creforce Operation Instruction No. 10 5 May 1941, issued 0200 hours, 4 May 1941. PRO WO 169/1334A, and contained with Laurie Barber and John Tonkin-Covell, *Freyberg, Churchill's Salamander* (London, United Kingdom: Century Hutchinson Ltd., 1990), 13-16.

APPENDIX G

CREFORCE ORDER OF BATTLE

CREFORCE HQ   Major-General Freyberg VC

1st Bn, Welch Regt

Máleme and Canea Sectors

HQ 2nd NZ Div   Acting Major-General Puttick
3rd Hussars (7 light tanks)

4th NZ Bde   Brigadier Inglis
18th Bn
19th Bn
1st Light Troop, RA

5th NZ Bde   Brigadier Hargest
7th Royal Tank Regt (2 Matilda tanks)
21st Bn
22nd Bn
23rd Bn
Engineer Det
28th (Maori) Bn
1st Greek Regt

10th NZ Bde   Colonel Kippenberger
NZ Div Cavalry
NZ Composite Bn
6th Greek Regt
8th Greek Regt
20th Bn (Div Reserve)

Suda Sector

Mobile Naval Base Defense Organisation   Major-General Weston
15th Coastal Defense Regt
Antiaircraft and Searchlight Bty
Marine Composite Bn
1st Bn Rangers
Northumberland Hussars
106th Royal Horse Artillery
16th Aust Inf Bde Composite Bn
17th Aust Inf Bde Composite Bn

'Royal Perivolians' Composite Bn
2nd Greek Regt

Geogioupolis

HQ 19th Aust Inf Bde   Brigadier Vasey
2nd/7th Aust Inf Bn
2nd/8th Aust Inf Bn

Retimo

2nd/1st Aust Inf Bn   Lieutenant-Colonel Campbell
2nd/11th Aust Inf Bn
7th Royal Tank Regt (2 Matilda tanks)
4th Greek Regt
5th Greek Regt
Cretan Gendarmerie

Heráklion Sector

HQ 14th Infantry Bde   Brigadier Chappel
2nd Bn, Black Watch
2nd Bn, York and Lancaster Regt
2nd Bn, Leicesters
2/4th Aust Inf Bn
7th Medium Regt, RA
7th Royal Tank Regt (2 Matilda tanks)
3rd Hussars (6 light tanks)
3rd Greek Regt
7th Greek Regt

Tymbaki

2nd Bn, Argyll and Sutherland Highlanders
7th Royal (2 Matilda tanks)

Strength

Total allied troops amounted to 42,460 of whom only about half were properly formed infantrymen. The total included about 9,000 Greek soldiers of whom only a small proportion, because of insufficient arms and training, played a significant role. In addition there were 1,200 Gendarmes and over 3,000 Cretan irregulars.

Source: Antony Beevor, *Crete: The Battle and the Resistance* (London, United Kingdom: John Murray Ltd., 1991), 345-346.

APPENDIX H

CREFORCE OPERATIONAL PLAN

> DUE TO COPYRIGHT RESTRICTIONS,
>
> IMAGES ARE NOT INCLUDED
>
> IN THIS ELECTRONIC EDITION.

Source: Davin, Daniel M. *Official History of New Zealand in the Second World War, 1939-45, Crete* (Wellington, New Zealand: War History Branch, 1953), pp. 97, 133, 151, 176, 177, 178.

BIBLIOGRAPHY

Ailsby, Christopher. *Hitler's Sky Warriors: German Paratroopers in Action, 1939-1945.* Dulles, VA: Brassey's, 2000.

Antill, Peter. *Crete 1941: Germany's Lightning Airborne Assault.* Botley, United Kingdom: Osprey Publishing, 2005.

Baldwin, Hanson W. *The Crucial Years 1939-1941.* New York: Harper and Row, 1976.

Barber, Laurie, and Tonkin-Covell, John. *Freyberg, Churchill's Salamander.* London, United Kingdom: Century Hutchinson Ltd., 1990.

Beevor, Antony. *Crete: The Battle and the Resistance.* London, United Kingdom: John Murray Ltd., 1991.

Bennett, Ralph. *Ultra and the Mediterranean Strategy.* New York: William Morrow and Company, 1989.

Buckley, Christopher. *Greece and Crete, 1941.* London, United Kingdom: Her Majesty's Stationary Office, 1952.

Calvocoressi, Peter. *Top Secret Ultra.* New York: Pantheon Books, 1980.

Churchill, Winston S. *The Second World War, Volume 3, The Grand Alliance.* Boston: Houghton Mifflin Company, 1950.

Clarke, Alan. *The Fall of Crete.* London, United Kingdom: Orion Publishing Co., 1963.

Comeau, Marcel G. *Operation Mercury: A British Airman's First-Hand Account of the Fall of Crete in 1941.* London, United Kingdom: Patrick Stephens Ltd., 1991.

Cox, Geoffrey. *A Tale of Two Battles: A Personal Memoir of Crete and the Western Desert, 1941.* London, United Kingdom: William Kimber and Co. Ltd., 1987.

Crawford, John. *Kia Kaha: New Zealand in the Second World War.* Auckland, New Zealand: Oxford University Press, 2000.

Davin, Daniel M. *Official History of New Zealand in the Second World War, 1939-45, Crete.* Wellington, New Zealand: War History Branch, 1953.

De Guingand, Francis. *Operation Victory.* New York: Charles Scribner's Sons, 1947.

Department of the Army. Pamphlet No. 20-260, *The German Campaigns in the Balkans (Spring 1941), Appendix II.* Washington, DC: Center of Military History, November 1953.

Ellis, Chris. *Spearhead No 3. 7th Flieger Division: Student's Fallschirmjäger Elite.* Hersham, United Kingdom: Ian Allen Publishing, 2002.

Farrar-Hockley, A .H. *Student.* New York: Ballantine Books Inc., 1973.

Freyberg, Paul. *Bernard Freyberg VC: Soldier of Two Nations.* Kent, United Kingdom: Hodder and Stoughton, 1991.

Garnett, David. *The Campaign in Greece and Crete.* London, United Kingdom: Great Britain War Office, H.M.S.O. 1942.

Haddon Donald. Interviewed by Sergeant Brenton Beach, 19 September 2001, interviews 3a, 3b, 4a, 4b, transcript, Queen Elizabeth II Army Memorial Museum Veterans Oral History Project, Waiouru, New Zealand.

Hetherington, John. *Airborne Invasion.* Auckland, New Zealand: Oswald-Sealy, 1944.

Hutching, Megan. *A Unique Sort of War: New Zealanders Remember Crete.* Auckland, New Zealand: HarperCollins, 2001.

Keegan, John. *Churchill's Generals.* New York: Quill William Morrow, 1991.

_____. *Intelligence in War: Knowledge of the Enemy from Napoleon to Al-Qaeda.* New York: Knopf, 2003.

Kippenberger, Howard Karl. *Infantry Brigadier.* London, United Kingdom: Oxford University Press, 1949.

Kiriakopoulos, G. C. *Ten Days to Destiny: The Battle for Crete, 1941.* New York: F. Watts, 1985.

Lewin, Ronald. *The Chief: Field Marshall Lord Wavell.* New York: Farrar Straus Giroux, 1980.

_____. *Ultra Goes to War.* New York: McGraw-Hill Books Company, 1978.

Liddell Hart, B. H. *The German Generals Talk.* New York: Quill William Morrow, 1948.

MacDonald, Callum. *The Lost Battle: Crete, 1941.* New York: Free Press, 1993.

McClymont, W. G. *Official History of New Zealand in the Second World War, 1939-45, To Greece.* Wellington, New Zealand: War History Branch, 1959.

New Zealand Army 2nd New Zealand Expeditionary Force. *Battle for Crete: The New Zealand Division in Action.* Wellington, New Zealand: Army Board, 1943.

Pitt, Barrie. *The Crucible of War I: Wavell's Command.* London, United Kingdom: Papermac, 1980.

Raugh, Harold E. *Wavell in the Middle East, 1939-1941: A Study in Generalship.* London, United Kingdom: Brassey's, 1993.

Shores, Christopher. *Air War for Yugoslavia, Greece and Crete.* London, United Kingdom: Grub Street, 1987.

Simpson, Tony. *Operation Mercury: The Battle for Crete, 1941.* London, United Kingdom: Hodder and Stroughton, 1981.

Spencer, John Hall. *Battle for Crete.* London, United Kingdom: Heinemann, 1962.

Stewart, Ian. *The Struggle for Crete: A Story of Lost Opportunity, 20 May–1 June 1941.* London, United Kingdom: Oxford University Press, 1966.

Student, Kurt. *Generaloberst Kurt Student und seine Fallschirmjäger.* Friedberg, Germany: Podzun-Pallas-Verlag, 1978.

Thomas, David. *Nazi Victory: Crete, 1941.* New York: Stein and Day, 1972.

Walker, Ernest. *The Price of Surrender: 1941: The War in Crete.* London, United Kingdom: Blandford, 1992.

White, John. Interviewed by Sergeant Brenton Beach, 8 March 2004, interview 3a, 3b, 7a, 7b, 8a, 8b, 9a, 9b, 10a, 10b, transcript, Queen Elizabeth II Army Memorial Museum Veterans Oral History Project, Waiouru, New Zealand.

Willingham, Matthew. *Perilous Commitments: Britain's Involvement in Greece and Crete 1940-41.* London, United Kingdom: Spellmount Publishers, 2004.

INITIAL DISTRIBUTION LIST

Combined Arms Research Library
U.S. Army Command and General Staff College
250 Gibbon Ave.
Fort Leavenworth, KS 66027-2314

Defense Technical Information Center/OCA
825 John J. Kingman Rd., Suite 944
Fort Belvoir, VA 22060-6218

Mr. Wilburn E. Meador
DMH
USACGSC
1 Reynolds Ave.
Fort Leavenworth, KS 66027-1352

Dr. Christopher Gabel
DMH
USACGSC
1 Reynolds Ave.
Fort Leavenworth, KS 66027-1352

Lieutenant Colonel Andrew F. Mahoney
CAL
USACGSC
1 Reynolds Ave.
Fort Leavenworth, KS 66027-1352

CERTIFICATION FOR MMAS DISTRIBUTION STATEMENT

1. Certification Date: 16 June 2006

2. Thesis Author: Major James C. Bliss

3. Thesis Title: The Fall of Crete 1941: Was Freyberg Culpable?

4. Thesis Committee Members: _____
   Signatures: _____
   _____

5. Distribution Statement: See distribution statements A-X on reverse, then circle appropriate distribution statement letter code below:

   (A) B C D E F X   SEE EXPLANATION OF CODES ON REVERSE

If your thesis does not fit into any of the above categories or is classified, you must coordinate with the classified section at CARL.

6. Justification: Justification is required for any distribution other than described in Distribution Statement A. All or part of a thesis may justify distribution limitation. See limitation justification statements 1-10 on reverse, then list, below, the statement(s) that applies (apply) to your thesis and corresponding chapters/sections and pages. Follow sample format shown below:

EXAMPLE

Limitation Justification Statement	/	Chapter/Section	/	Page(s)
Direct Military Support (10)	/	Chapter 3	/	12
Critical Technology (3)	/	Section 4	/	31
Administrative Operational Use (7)	/	Chapter 2	/	13-32

Fill in limitation justification for your thesis below:

Limitation Justification Statement	/	Chapter/Section	/	Page(s)
_____	/	_____	/	_____
_____	/	_____	/	_____
_____	/	_____	/	_____
_____	/	_____	/	_____
_____	/	_____	/	_____

7. MMAS Thesis Author's Signature: _____

STATEMENT A: Approved for public release; distribution is unlimited. (Documents with this statement may be made available or sold to the general public and foreign nationals).

STATEMENT B: Distribution authorized to U.S. Government agencies only (insert reason and date ON REVERSE OF THIS FORM). Currently used reasons for imposing this statement include the following:

    1. Foreign Government Information. Protection of foreign information.

    2. Proprietary Information. Protection of proprietary information not owned by the U.S. Government.

    3. Critical Technology. Protection and control of critical technology including technical data with potential military application.

    4. Test and Evaluation. Protection of test and evaluation of commercial production or military hardware.

    5. Contractor Performance Evaluation. Protection of information involving contractor performance evaluation.

    6. Premature Dissemination. Protection of information involving systems or hardware from premature dissemination.

    7. Administrative/Operational Use. Protection of information restricted to official use or for administrative or operational purposes.

    8. Software Documentation. Protection of software documentation - release only in accordance with the provisions of DoD Instruction 7930.2.

    9. Specific Authority. Protection of information required by a specific authority.

    10. Direct Military Support. To protect export-controlled technical data of such military significance that release for purposes other than direct support of DoD-approved activities may jeopardize a U.S. military advantage.

STATEMENT C: Distribution authorized to U.S. Government agencies and their contractors: (REASON AND DATE). Currently most used reasons are 1, 3, 7, 8, and 9 above.

STATEMENT D: Distribution authorized to DoD and U.S. DoD contractors only; (REASON AND DATE). Currently most reasons are 1, 3, 7, 8, and 9 above.

STATEMENT E: Distribution authorized to DoD only; (REASON AND DATE). Currently most used reasons are 1, 2, 3, 4, 5, 6, 7, 8, 9, and 10.

STATEMENT F: Further dissemination only as directed by (controlling DoD office and date), or higher DoD authority. Used when the DoD originator determines that information is subject to special dissemination limitation specified by paragraph 4-505, DoD 5200.1-R.

STATEMENT X: Distribution authorized to U.S. Government agencies and private individuals of enterprises eligible to obtain export-controlled technical data in accordance with DoD Directive 5230.25; (date). Controlling DoD office is (insert).

www.ingramcontent.com/pod-product-compliance
Lightning Source LLC
Chambersburg PA
CBHW080920170426
43201CB00016B/2204